REAL FOCUS

Take control and start living
the life you want

PSYCHOLOGIES
MAGAZINE

Library of Congress Cataloging-in-Publication Data

Title: Real focus : take control and start living the life you want / Psychologies Magazine.
Description: Chichester, West Sussex, United Kingdom : John Wiley & Sons,
    2016. | Includes bibliographical references.
Identifiers: LCCN 2016006352| ISBN 9780857086600 (pbk.)
Subjects: LCSH: Time management. | Distraction (Psychology) | Attention.
Classification: LCC BF637.T5 R43 2016 | DDC 650.1–dc23 LC record available at
    http://lccn.loc.gov/2016006352

A catalogue record for this book is available from the British Library.

ISBN 978-0-857-08660-0 (pbk) ISBN 978-0-857-08661-7 (ebk)
ISBN 978-0-857-08662-4 (ebk)

Cover Design: Wiley

Set in 9.5/13 ITC Franklin Gothic Std by Aptara

Printed in Great Britain by TJ International Ltd, Padstow, Cornwall, UK

CONTENTS

FOREWORD

by Suzy Greaves, Editor, Psychologies

Time is the currency of our lives. We are all given the same amount of time to spend – 8760 hours a year, 730 hours a month, 168 hours a week – so how are we choosing to spend that time? Your ability to focus, be it giving the full beam of your attention to the people you love or delivering an important project at work, can mean the difference between a happy, productive life and a lost, miserable one.

That's why I love this book. It helps you discover the key to spending your time consciously and wisely instead of frittering days away on reacting to the assault of never-ending demands – which means you'll be free to proactively create the life you *really* want.

At *Psychologies*, our slogan on the front of the magazine is 'your life, your way'. Our readers are passionate about creating a life that works for them on their own terms. But, as we all know, that's difficult to do when we find ourselves distracted, overwhelmed and frazzled. How can you even begin to ask the bigger questions (*What do I want? Where am I going? What do I want to create?*) when you're squashed flat under a giant to-do list? This book encourages you to create the space and time to identify what really is stealing your time and attention so you can create a strategy to focus on what really matters to you – with the help of the most renowned and respected productivity experts in the world.

I believe this book will not only save you time but quite literally save your life – one minute at a time. Are you ready? OK, let's focus.

Suzy Greaves, Editor, *Psychologies*

INTRODUCTION

How are you today? We would hazard a guess that your answer will be along the lines of 'I'm so busy', 'I feel so frazzled', or 'what am I doing even reading this book, I've got so much to do!'

However, we also suspect that you know in your heart of hearts that life's not supposed to feel like this. You're not supposed to feel like you're in a hamster wheel that you can't get off; that life is a 'whirlwind' or 'one never-ending to-do list'. You know there has to be another way – but what is it?

Well here it is: Real Focus. We suspect that the reason you're reading this book is because you feel your lack of focus is causing you problems in your life. Perhaps you feel overwhelmed by how much you have to do every day in the time available; or you're unclear about your goals and what you really want. Maybe you're sick of getting to the end of another 'manic' day and thinking: what have I actually achieved?

You probably look at other people and think they've got it all worked out (we can pretty much guarantee, they haven't). At the end of the day though, this isn't about anyone else, it's about you; it's about creating a life that allows you the time and space to do everything that matters, and spend time with those that matter too. We feel that's what Real Focus is, in a nutshell: doing what matters. It's kind of simple and yet tricky all at the same time.

The good news is that anybody can achieve it when they know how; and this book is the first step.

HOW TO USE THIS BOOK

First of all, it's important that you use this book in the way that benefits you the most. All we want is for you to take away as much as possible to help you in your personal journey towards better focus. To that end, we've split this book into three, clear sections so that you can dip in and out, read from front to back, or in whichever way you wish.

Part One is called *How Focused Are You?* This section will help you to look at how you feel now (how your lack of focus might be affecting your life), and what life could look and feel like if your focus improved. We have also put together a list of what we, at *Psychologies*, feel constitutes Real Focus. It's meant as a helpful list of goals if you like, but you can add to and omit as you see fit, curating your own personal set of goals. Perhaps you'll want to stick our list up on your fridge, or use it as inspiration for your own.

Part Two is called *Why Do You Lack Focus?* Covering key issues like time management and work/life balance, this section will help you to identify the issues that might be standing in the way of you reaching your potential and hindering your efforts to become more focused.

Part Three is called *How Can You Become More Focused?* Taking everything we have learned and explored throughout the book, this section is packed full of tips and strategies for you to 'practise' Real Focus and keep practising long after you have finished this book. Like any life skill, 'Real Focus' is something you need to keep at; you don't master it overnight. However, there are plenty of bite-sized tips throughout the book, so that you can start working on your focus straightaway.

You will also find tests that will help you assess yourself and navigate your personal journey towards Real Focus. We hope that these, along with the 'Ask Yourself' questions at the end of each chapter, will help you to gain a deeper understanding of your obstacles and goals where focus is concerned and also to relate what you read in this book to your own experience. In addition, we have included case studies from real people (names and identifying circumstances changed). Their journeys will help you see how it's possible to achieve Real Focus and give you a wider range of tools to do so yourself.

We interviewed a sociologist, a clinical psychologist/mindfulness expert, a time management and productivity expert, an investigative journalist, an entrepreneur/business author and a speaker/author. All of them are leaders in their field and were handpicked by us to offer as varied and rounded a picture as possible of what Real Focus is and how you can achieve it. For all their colourful differences, however, it could be said that they all have one, clear goal: to help people to live a 'good life' – that is, a balanced, happy, full life that is rich with the things that matter to them. They are united in the fact that in order to make this possible, one must cultivate Real Focus. We hope that, contained within these pages, is how.

THE EXPERTS INTERVIEWED FOR *REAL FOCUS*

Dalton Conley, sociologist, Henry Putnam University Professor of Sociology at Princeton University

Dalton has many academic roles including University Dean, University Professor and Research Associate at the National Bureau of Economic Research. He writes and speaks on subjects such as race, socioeconomic status, poverty and the role of technology in society. He coined the term 'weisure' to describe the blurring of work and leisure and is also the author of many books, including *Social Class: How Does it Work?*, *Elsewhere USA* and his latest, *Parentology*.

@daltonconley

Mark Forster, author and specialist in time management and organization

Mark is the author of numerous books including *Get Everything Done*, *Do It Tomorrow and Other Secrets of Time Management* and *Still Have Time To Play*. His latest book is *Secrets of Productive People*. Mark has also developed a time-management system called Final Version.

http://markforster.squarespace.com/home/
@AutofocusTM

Dr Tamara Russell, clinical psychologist, mindfulness trainer and martial artist

Tamara combines all three disciplines to work with individuals and organizations advising on mindfulness techniques to enhance performance and improve mental and physical wellbeing. She is director of the Mindfulness Centre of Excellence (virtual) and author of *Mindfulness in Motion* (Watkins Publishing), a book teaching the Body In Mind training which she developed.

www.drtamararussell.com

Brigid Schulte, author, former award-winning *Washington Post* reporter and current director of The Better Life Lab at the nonprofit think tank, New America, and mother of two

A few years ago, Brigid found herself besieged by constant, exhausting busyness. Wondering why she felt so overwhelmed, she decided to go on a quest to find out. The result is her *New York Times* bestseller: *Overwhelmed: How to Work, Love, and Play When No one Has The Time* (Picador). Schulte was a long-time, award-winning journalist for The Washington Post, and now directs the Better Life Lab at New America, which seeks to drive the evolution of work, reframe gender equality to include both the advance of women and the changing roles of men, and rewire policy to support the needs of diverse 21st century families.

www.brigidschulte.com
@BrigidSchulte

Laura Vanderkam, author and speaker on topics such as time, money and productivity

Laura questions the status quo and helps people to rediscover their true passions and beliefs in pursuit of more meaningful lives. Her books include *What the Most Successful People Do Before Breakfast* (Portfolio), *168 Hours: You Have More Time Than You Think* (Portfolio), and *All the Money in the World: What the Happiest People Know About Wealth* (Portfolio). Her latest book is *I Know How She Does It: How Successful Women Make the Most of Their Time* (Portfolio). She is also a frequent contributor to Fast Company's website and a member of USA Today's Board of Contributors.

www.lauravanderkam.com
@lvanderkam

Sháá Wasmund, MBE, speaker, entrepreneur and author

Sháá is one of the UK's most prominent female entrepreneurs and a champion of small businesses. After being a boxing manager (the only woman ever to do so), she set up Smarta.com, which gives advice and tools to small businesses and start ups. In 2015, she was awarded an MBE for services to business and entrepreneurship. She is also the author of the bestselling books *Stop Talking, Start Doing* and *Do Less, Get More*.

www.shaa.com
@shaawasmund

1 HOW FOCUSED ARE YOU?

CHAPTER 1

DEFINING 'REAL FOCUS'

HOW DO YOU FEEL RIGHT NOW?

So what is 'Real Focus' anyway? Why do you need it and what would it bring to your life? In order to start answering these questions, we need to look at how your life probably feels right now – in other words, what Real Focus definitely *isn't*.

Chances are if you feel Real Focus is a problem for you, the following phrases feature heavily in your vocabulary:

'Life's just crazy …'

'There aren't enough hours in the day …'

'I'm feeling totally overwhelmed …'

'Stop, I want to get off!'

One of the key characteristics of lacking focus and feeling overwhelmed is that we can't see the wood for the trees. This feels slightly different for everybody, but we'd put money on the fact that the following are very familiar …

1. Your time feels fragmented and 'bitty'

Brigid Schulte, harassed mother of two and reporter for the *Washington Post*, remembers very clearly the point at which she decided she had to write her book *Overwhelmed: How To Work, Love, and Play When No One Has The Time*. She was clearing up after her son's birthday party and her husband was outside on the patio smoking a cigar. She'd cleared the food and plates away and all that was left to do now was to sweep the 'Happy Birthday' confetti off the table and floor. As an exhausted Schulte surveyed the small bits and pieces all over the place, it occurred to her that her life felt exactly like the confetti: scattered, fragmented and exhausting.

Sound familiar? When we're trying to stretch ourselves too far, we lose sight of our goals and feel overwhelmed. This is how our time feels: like hundreds of little pieces of confetti – that when you put them back together don't seem to amount to much. You feel like you've been on your feet all day, completing endless tasks: sending emails, running errands, and working your way through an ever-expanding to-do list – but do you feel like you've actually achieved anything?

Of course, you're not alone in feeling like this. Our harried lives and constant busyness seem to have overtaken the weather as the UK's number one topic of conversation. We have more choice than ever in terms of what we do with our time, but this is stressing us out even more because we don't know what to focus on. As a result, we fall into the trap of trying to focus on everything, splintering ourselves and our time into a million pieces of 'time confetti'.

This goes not just for work but for family and leisure time too. It's probable that you feel like you don't have enough down time and that it's difficult to get any unbroken periods of relaxation when your day is so fragmented. But the thing is, this down time is actually always in reach – you just need to learn how to find it.

This book will not change 'time'. There will always be 24 hours in a day and 168 hours in a week. What it will help you with, however, is how you manage and therefore experience time, so that things feel more focused and you feel calmer and, ultimately, happier. Schulte calls it moving from 'time confetti' to 'time serenity'. Imagine …

BRIGID SCHULTE ON THE PROBLEM WITH 'TIME CONFETTI'

'When I saw that confetti whilst clearing up after my son's birthday party, I knew that's exactly how life can feel: all these little bits and scraps of time that don't amount to much of anything.

Psychologists who have studied time and how we spend it, have found that we are happiest when we are in flow – that is, focusing on something for an uninterrupted period of time and being engrossed in it. However, our time is so fragmented these days, and we're so busy, it's often hard to find that stretch of time in the first place. And even if we could, we struggle to give ourselves permission to really sink into flow. We get distracted by our To Do list, we're worried about being "productive." And without taking time to think about what's most important, we often don't really know what to focus on, or where to start. It takes practice, especially practice in giving ourselves permission to experience flow.

But research is showing very clearly that we can't multi-task like this and expect to do everything well. Instead of multi-tasking, we're really task-switching, which wears out the brain and degrades focus and attention, so you end up not doing anything particularly well. And in the end, that just makes us feel worse.'

FOCUS ON ONE THING

If you're having trouble focusing, decide on the ONE thing you have to do by a certain time: It could be by the end of the day, or the end of the hour. The important thing is, don't do anything else until you've done it.

2. You feel like you're constantly trying to do several things at once

Multi-tasking. It used to be seen as a virtue, didn't it? Something to be proud of. Taking a call whilst jotting down a to-do list? Well done you. Firing off quick emails during a meeting? Practising your presentation whilst driving into town? Two birds with one stone! Maybe you still look at multi-taskers in awe. If you ask most people, however, (including yourself) we bet they'd say in practise that multi-tasking is something they feel they have to do rather than choose to do, and that it only adds to their feelings of being overwhelmed.

> **" Do the right thing at the right time, rather than trying to do everything all of the time. "**
>
> Sháá Wasmund, MBE, speaker, entrepreneur and author

If you look up the term 'multi-tasking' on Wikipedia, it tells you that the term itself derives from 'computer multi-tasking' (where the computer performs multiple tasks concurrently). It entered our vocabularies in the late nineties, early noughties. It was a time when the Information Age was just beginning, and there was a definite feeling of 'more is more' and 'faster is better'. This could explain why 'multi-tasking' had much more positive connotations back then.

But now, 15 or more years later, could we be finally waking up to the multi-tasking myth? Could it be that doing several things at once doesn't actually make us more focused and productive and that, in fact, the opposite is true? Scientists and academics certainly seem to think so.

Researchers at Stanford University[1] compared groups of people based on their tendency to multi-task and their belief that it helps their performance. They found that heavy multi-taskers – those who multi-task a lot and feel that it boosts their performance – were actually worse at multi-tasking than those who like to do a single thing at a time. The frequent multi-taskers performed worse because they had more trouble organizing their thoughts and filtering out irrelevant information, and they were slower at switching from one task to another.

In short, multi-tasking reduces your efficiency and performance, because your brain can only focus on one thing at a time.

TRAVIS BRADBERRY ON THE INEFFICIENCY OF MULTI-TASKING

'Besides making you less efficient, researchers also found that multi-tasking actually lowers your IQ. A study at the University of London found that participants who multi-tasked during cognitive tasks experienced IQ score declines that were similar to what they'd expect if they had smoked marijuana or stayed up all night.'

Sourced from 'Multitasking Damages Your Brain And Career, New Studies Suggest', Dr Travis Bradberry, *Forbes* magazine, http://www.forbes.com/sites/travisbradberry/2014/10/08/multitasking-damages-your-brain-and-career-new-studies-suggest/

Something to tell the kids when they're trying to do their homework in front of the TV at least?

❝No two tasks done simultaneously can be done with a 100 per cent of one's attention.❞

Brigid Schulte, author of *Overwhelmed*

We know it sometimes feels irresistible, not to mention unavoidable, to do several things at once. We also know that multi-tasking doesn't have to mean doing several tasks at once; it can also mean *being* several things at once. Role-switching is something we're going to look at in more detail later on, but now we'll just say this: this book is about finding Real Focus. We hope you're convinced that in order to do that, it's better to do one thing at a time. There, you see? Easy. You've probably improved your focus no end already just with that one small promise to yourself.

3. You feel like life is a series of interruptions and distractions

That's possibly because it is. From the constant ping of messages and Facebook updates, to the seemingly unavoidable distractions like phone-calls and meetings, there are constant demands on our attention. The Internet is a wonderful thing, but with 24/7 access to it, news channels and addiction to social media, we are constantly bombarded with information in a way we weren't even 20 years ago. It's got to the point now where sociologists are calling it an official 'Crisis of Attention', because there are so many things we could focus on, we don't know which are important anymore. We've lost the art of concentration.

> ❝Every time you are distracted from one task by something or someone else it takes an average of eleven minutes to get your focus back.❞
>
> Sháá Wasmund, MBE, speaker, entrepreneur and author

This book can't rewind the technological age and eradicate Facebook and Twitter (although you probably sometimes wish it could). What this book hopes to do, however, is suggest ways you might manage these constant distractions – even eradicate some. We hope to empower you with the ability to switch off from what isn't important so that you can focus on what is.

REAL PEOPLE
"How I found my focus" – *Debbie*

'I am a freelance copywriter so am responsible for finding and maintaining my own clients and have to manage my time. It had been going well for about five years until things started to spin out of control shortly after my two daughters went to school full time. Despite having more time on my hands with my kids being at school, I found I had less structure to my days, not more.

I began to struggle with self-discipline and focus and also the isolation of working alone. If I didn't "catch" my best hours in the morning, I found I could easily squander a whole day procrastinating – telling myself I'd get down to work after

I'd booked this, or been to do a supermarket shop or taken a call from a friend. I'd then feel terribly guilty and spend all evening working to make up for it, forfeiting time I could spend doing something I enjoyed, or with my girls.

I realized something had to change when I basically ran out of money. My lack of focus meant I wasn't earning what I needed and this in turn, made me feel pressured, depressed and even more distracted. I had to do something! It was talking to a mixture of friends, other freelancers and a coach that helped me come up with strategies:

- I got into a habit of doing a 10-minute mindfulness exercise (using "Headspace") every morning, and taking regular exercise classes on regular days.
- I started working in the local library to build in a structure of "going" somewhere to work, which helped enormously to focus me.
- Internet access at the library requires requesting a code, which I purposefully avoided doing. This gave me a few hours of completely focused time.
- I would check my emails in the morning and only answer essential messages, then I would work in the library and not check emails again until lunchtime – again only responding to the absolute essentials.
- I switched my phone off to remove the constant distraction of every beep, every call, every text. Instead I checked it regularly every couple of hours.

All the structure meant I got more done. In turn, this meant my motivation soared which meant I got more done still! It just took me realizing there was a problem and actually sitting down and making decisions about how to solve it that helped in the end.'

4. You feel like you're constantly busy but achieving nothing

We suspect that if we asked you how busy you were, your response would be *face-aghast* 'Are you kidding? You've NO IDEA!' It's become our standard response, almost as though if you're not seen to be permanently frantic, there must be something wrong.

Of course, we're all gripped by a busyness epidemic. You only need to try and organize a social with your friends and be told 'Love to! But my next free weekend isn't until four months' time' to know that. You're so busy, but have you ever stopped to ask yourself what you're busy doing exactly? What 'busy' means, in reality, for you? And above all, what is all the busyness achieving?

The key to looking at this might be first to come to a better understanding of what 'busy' actually means. The dictionary definition says 'engaged in activity'. But is this the same thing as productive? Focused?

MARK FORSTER ON THE DIFFERENCE BETWEEN 'REAL WORK' AND 'BUSY WORK'

In his book Secrets of Productive People, *Forster explains that one of the most basic distinctions we need to make in our lives if we want to be focused and productive, is the difference between 'action and activity'.*

> *'Real work is the work that progresses our goals, visions, career. Busy work is what we do in order to avoid real work. Another way of putting it is that real work is action, while busy work is merely activity.'*

In short, the thing to remember is that with action you have something to show for it – for example, booking a holiday; whereas with an activity you don't – spending hours browsing on the Internet for one, for example. We hope this book will help you to have something to show for your efforts more often than not. And we don't just mean work projects or meeting deadlines, we mean achieving your dreams, nurturing your relationships and generally leading a more full and balanced life.

HOW WOULD YOU LIKE TO FEEL?

We've ascertained what you might be feeling like right now, the reason perhaps that you are reading this book. Now we need to move on to how you would like to feel. What do people with Real Focus do that you don't? What habits do they have? Here at *Psychologies* we've boiled it down to the following list – but, obviously, you can amend, add to, or take from it to suit your interpretation:

- Real Focus is 'curating' the best life for you: knowing what's important to you – doing less, but more of the things that matter.
- Real Focus is playing to your strengths and doing what you love.
- Real Focus is devoting time to thinking about how to change things.
- Real Focus is not overcommitting yourself.
- Real Focus is giving regular, focused attention to the things you want to happen.
- Real Focus is having systems.
- Real Focus is you having time to work, love and play.

Perhaps you'll be on your way to achieving all of these, some of these or only one of these by the end of reading this book. What matters is that you've identified that you want things to change and you've started the ball rolling.

DR TAMARA RUSSELL ON USING MINDFULNESS FOR BETTER FOCUS

'In mindfulness, you are training your attention, but an important part of doing that is the training in the detection of inattention – that is, when your mind starts to wander. Sometimes people use external objects to hold their attention, or they simply try to concentrate on their breath or their thoughts. This is fine, but training objects have different levels of ability to hold our attention and trying to observe your thoughts, for example, can be very difficult as they are not very tangible. They're difficult to "hold onto". If you are asked to concentrate on walking, however, then this is much easier. There is a much richer array of sensations to hold your attention and you can notice more quickly when focus has been lost.

This is where Body in Mind training (a framework developed by myself) comes in. You are using the body as the main training object for the mind. The body itself and the movement of the body supports the training of attention, giving you something to hold onto. In turn this helps you in the following three domains:

1. It lessens the impact of distraction. Not that you never get distracted again, but you recognize sooner when this happens and spend less time distracted.

2. Because attention and emotion are linked in the brain, if you train attention, it will impact on your ability to cope better with your emotions too; to notice them and "be" with them instead of trying to escape them. The body is a particularly useful tool here as we often feel or sense emotional states in the body.

3. Your interpersonal skills improve. Because you are more aware of your feelings, you are also more aware of other

people's, of the fact we're all feeling the same. You're much better able to connect with people and be there for them. You realize it's not "all about me".

Two exercises for Body in Mind training:

1. *Mindful walking: You can do this anywhere, walking along the street or in the park. Just pay attention to the sensations in your body: the feelings of the soles of the feet hitting the floor, the feeling of the muscles, the bones; whether anything hurts or where there's tension or relaxation.*

2. *Mindful sitting: If you feel you are lacking focus when you're working, just take a moment to bring the attention back to the body in its sitting position: How does your bum feel on the chair? Your back against it? Notice any heat or pressure; whether there's tension in the shoulders or spine and what muscles you're using to hold your body in that sitting position. You're training your mind and its ability to focus by using your body.'*

ASK YOURSELF

 Define what Real Focus means to you.

Identify areas in your life where you think you have it.

Identify areas in your life where you think you don't.

 What are the main symptoms of your lack of focus (i.e. constantly late, feeling paralysed and overwhelmed, disorganized)?

How do you feel about tackling these now?

HOW FOCUSED ARE YOU?

If you never feel like you achieve enough in the day, despite being convinced that you're working harder than ever, it's time to look at what's undermining your focus and productivity. There are more demands on our attention these days than ever before, and it's not always easy to filter out the constant interruptions that have become part of modern life. Finding the right balance can be a case of trial and error to craft an approach that works for you. Take our quiz to find out what's undermining your focus, and what changes you need to make to protect your valuable mental resources.

Test by Sally Brown

QUESTION 1

You sit down at your screen to do some work. How long is it before you break off to check your email, social media or browse the internet?

A. Every couple of minutes. I multi-task and switch between screens
B. Probably every 10 or 15 minutes or so
C. I avoid looking until I've finished the work I need to do

QUESTION 2

Rate your default stress levels in an average day:

A. I have my moments, but most of the time I feel calm
B. I feel stressed at work, but I usually manage to leave it behind
C. Most days I feel constantly frazzled

QUESTION 3

Which of these statements describes your typical day?

A. I feel like I'm constantly firefighting problems and dealing with interruptions
B. I spend so much time sorting out admin and small stuff I don't get round to what's important
C. I devote chunks of time to really focus on the biggest tasks of the day

---

QUESTION 4

You sit down to watch a film with the family. Do you:

A. Watch while scrolling through your Facebook and Twitter feed on your phone
B. Leave your phone in another room and focus on the film
C. Put your phone down but pick it up if it beeps

QUESTION 5

When was the last time you experienced 'flow' (feeling so immersed in what you're doing that you lose track of time)?

A. In the last few days
B. It's been so long I can't honestly remember
C. Around a month ago

QUESTION 6

Which statement do you most agree with?

A. I have so much to do I've lost sight of what I need to focus on
B. I have a list of priorities for every day and I stick to them
C. I start off the day focused but get distracted by tasks that come up

---

QUESTION 7

What's your favourite way of taking a break during the day?

A. Ringing or texting a friend
B. Scrolling through Facebook or online shopping sites
C. Going for a brisk walk, even for just ten minutes

QUESTION 8

How would you rate your memory?

A. Generally pretty good
B. Terrible – if I don't write things down, I forget them
C. OK, but definitely not as good as it used to be

QUESTION 9

How do you usually feel at the end of the working day?

A. Satisfied that I've worked hard and ready to relax
B. A bit frazzled but like I've achieved most of the things I wanted to
C. Exhausted and feeling like I haven't really accomplished anything

---

QUESTION 10

Set a timer for three minutes, then close your eyes and focus on your breathing. Rate how you found it:

A. Frustrating – I never knew three minutes could last so long
B. OK, my mind kept wandering but I felt more relaxed afterwards
C. Good – it's something I do regularly throughout the day to refresh my focus

Now, add up your scores from each answer, and find out how focused you are below:

	A	B	C
Q1	1	2	3
Q2	3	2	1
Q3	1	2	3
Q4	1	3	2
Q5	3	1	2
Q6	1	3	2
Q7	2	1	3
Q8	3	1	2
Q9	3	2	1
Q10	1	2	3

If you scored between 10 and 18...

Distracted is your Default state

It's no wonder you've picked up this book – you know something has to change! Your time feels fragmented, peppered with constant interruptions, so you never get a chance to finish anything. You often feel frazzled and exhausted by the end of the day, but find it hard to relax as there still seems to be so much to do. You may have also fallen into the multi-tasking trap so that even when you get a chance to work interrupted, you find it impossible to resist checking your emails or social media. You will find lots of practical tips and advice in the rest of the book to help you reconnect with your ability to concentrate, but introducing a daily 10-minute mindfulness exercise is a great way to start. It's also worth considering a digital detox day once a week.

If you scored between 19 and 24...

You struggle to Focus

You haven't lost the ability to focus, but sometimes you lose sight of it, by getting sucked into multi-tasking and feeling 'busy'. You're coping, but at times, you feel like your head is overflowing with information and your memory can be patchy. The good news is that small changes can make a big difference. Try identifying your 'golden hour', the time when you're at your most productive (it's often first thing in the morning). Ring-fence it to focus on what really matters, by turning off email and social media, and avoiding meetings if you can. It can help set the tone for the rest of the day. And read on for more practical ways to reset your focus.

If you scored between 25 and 30...

You're a focus Ninja

It's not easy to resist the 24-7 onslaught of information, but you have managed to find a balance that works most of the time, by prioritizing what's most important to you. You've wised up to the fact that multi-tasking and being perpetually busy isn't good for productivity or mental health. The pay-off is regular feelings of flow and a high level of wellbeing. You may wonder if you need to read on, but be aware that focus can be fragile. The practical resources and support offered in the following chapters will help you build resilience against future distractions.

CHAPTER 2

THE BUSY TRAP

SO WHAT IS THE BUSY TRAP AND HAVE YOU FALLEN INTO IT?

e've talked about the difference between busyness and focus/activity and action, but let's look a little deeper at the epidemic of busyness. How come we've fallen prey to it and what is it doing to our focus? There are many reasons why people stay on the hamster wheel or meander through life not achieving what they want, but a common one, say psychologists, is fear.

But fear of what?

One of the keys to Real Focus is asking yourself the right questions, so an important question to start with is: what am I scared of? What is stopping me living the life I want?

Don't be too hard on yourself though. Often the things we really want and that really matter to us are the most difficult to achieve. We need Real Focus if we're to have a chance, but it's a Catch 22: really focusing on our goals often means facing our fears and taking a big leap into the unknown – so what do we do? We keep busy instead, doing everything else to avoid facing our fears.

An author friend of mine once received the following message from a wannabe writer:

'I've been thinking of a career in writing for 40 years, but marriage/ family/social life always got in the way. Could we meet for coffee to discuss what's involved? I've heard it's hard work!'

My friend politely wrote back to say that if this woman really wanted to be a writer, she'd need to find a way of carving out the time and guarding it with her life – otherwise she'd run the risk of it never happening.

It was perhaps a rather naïve email to send and an extreme example, but that woman may genuinely have wanted to be a writer, yet have been caught in the 'busy trap' – for 40 years! – keeping busy, so she didn't have to face the fear of attempting to make her dreams come true and all the possibility of failure, humiliation and financial ruin that brings.

So how can you tell whether you're actually focused, or simply stuck in the busy trap? After all, the two can seem confusingly similar.

MARK FORSTER ON THE 'SYMPTOMS' OF BUSYNESS

'1. You overcommit yourself.

People can be very protective of their workload. It seems to be part of people's self-image that they're busy and it's very hard for them to give up stuff – in fact they usually want to know how to do even more! Everyone wants to look good and busy but you have to ask yourself: are you using busyness as a defence against stuff you don't want to do? Or that feels too hard?

2. You do all the easy stuff first – then make some more up.

If you have four tasks to do and one is very, very difficult, one is very difficult, one is just difficult and one is quite easy, which are you likely to start with? Most people will start with the easy one but this is a trap, because after you've done the easy one you are then even less likely to do the hardest one. What happens then is that the hardest one (the most important) gets pushed back down the list again and again with even less chance of it ever getting done. In fact, after you have completed the easy task, a big symptom of the busy trap is to invent more easy stuff to do to put off doing the difficult one!

3. You don't feel stretched but you do feel overwhelmed.

Ask yourself, are you working to the best of your abilities? Or just working all the time?

4. If you're working efficiently, you find yourself in a state of flow, because what you're doing is what you're meant to do.

It's what you're good at and what you enjoy. A sign you're not in flow but in the busy trap is a lot of procrastination, stress and chasing deadlines. You're exhausted but you've not much to show for it. That's the big difference between productivity and busyness – with the latter, there isn't much "return".'

THE BIG GLASS JAR THESIS

We've established that focusing isn't easy, that it takes, well … focus. We've also established that the flipside of focus is the comfort zone – or to put it another way, keeping busy to avoid facing your fears.

One way of helping yourself out of the busy trap and towards Real Focus is to do the difficult things first. To do this, we can use Mark Forster's 'big, glass jar analogy':

1. First you picture a big glass jar and fill it with sand.
2. You then try to add some big stones, but find that you can't because it's filled with sand.
3. Instead then, you add the stones first, before adding the sand.
4. Now you'll find that the sand fits itself around the stones.

You should take this same approach to your tasks – you should look to do the big, important stuff first and you'll find that the other stuff will fit its way around.

> ❗ ## SET ASIDE A DEDICATED EMAIL PERIOD
>
> **Set aside two half hours – one at the beginning of the day and one at the end – to read and reply to emails. You'll find most things are not so urgent they can't wait the period in between.**

ARE YOU A BUSY BRAGGER?

So, fear keeps us in the busy trap and stops us achieving Real Focus; but academics believe that cultural expectations also play a big part.

As part of writing her book, *Overwhelmed: How To Work, Love and Play When No one Has the Time*, Schulte met academic Ann Burnett who was studying busyness and how language creates our reality. Burnett had organized a focus group on busyness in Fargo, Dakota, near the Canadian border. As part of her studies, Burnett had collected people's Christmas holiday letters – ones people had sent to her, as well as ones she collected from friends – and scrutinized them for language surrounding busyness. What she found was startling: the letters read as 'brag sheets', Burnett reported, exercises on who can sound the busiest: 'Our schedules have always been crazy but now they're even crazier!' wrote one, 'I don't know where my time goes!' said another. What this seemed to show was that what people were really communicating was that they had earned a badge of honour for living in fast forward.

So people actually brag about how busy they are – maybe you even do it yourself. But why? Because busyness has become a cultural expectation and, according to sociologists, human beings generally like to follow social expectations even when they don't make sense or bring them what they really want in their lives.

What did Burnett make of the content of those letters? They demonstrate, she said, that we risk living in a state of 'forfeiture'– a lack of self-awareness from being so distracted by the hectic busyness in everyday life.

Since we only get one life that would be a crying shame, no?

SHÁÁ WASMUND ON THE 'U' RULE OF HAPPINESS

'Recent research (from the Royal Economic Society) has found that most people's lifetime happiness curve is U shaped: High in our youth, starts to trail off by the time we are 25 and doesn't pick up again until we retire. This suggests that, actually, we are much happier when life is simpler and when we're less busy, not more.'

So yes, we can be a perverse lot, us humans, but the U rule completely contradicts our busy bragging! Why show off about our schedules, if they make us miserable? It's counter-intuitive, which is why social commentators call it The Busy Trap.

TRY THE POMODORO TECHNIQUE FOR ULTIMATE FOCUS

Work for 25 minutes (set a timer) then have a 5 minute break and repeat six times. Nothing is that bad you can't concentrate solely on it for 25 minutes and, at the end, you'll have done two and a half hours of completely focused work.

> **"The key to productivity is regular focused attention. If you give a project those three things, it will move."**
>
> Mark Forster, author and specialist in time management and organization

BUSYNESS: ARE YOU DOING IT TO YOURSELF?

Writing in the *New York Times*,[1] Tom Kreider made the point that the busy trap is entirely one we've set for ourselves for the purpose of making us feel important.

> *'Busyness serves as a kind of existential reassurance ... obviously your life cannot possibly be trivial or meaningless if you are so busy.'*

However, Kreider makes the point that it's not generally those working three jobs on the minimum wage that complain of busyness (those, he says, are not busy, they're 'dead on their feet, exhausted'). It's those who organize endless activities and lessons for their children, or voluntarily take on extra work and obligations (secretary of the rugby club, rotary club social sec – anyone?). In other words, those whose busyness is self-imposed, through ambition of keeping up with the Joneses or because they 'dread what they might have to face in its absence'.

> **"The only way we can begin to see another way more clearly is if we give ourselves space."**
>
> Brigid Schulte, author of *Overwhelmed*

It's also well documented that the way we talk about our busyness and the language we use affects our experience of time and our perception of how 'busy we are' – this, sociologists call 'evidence based bias'.

LAURA VANDERKAM ON PERCEPTIONS OF BUSYNESS

'If we say all the time 'I'm so stressed out and have no time' we find evidence of that. But if we say 'actually my life is pretty awesome', and are defined by what is good in our lives rather than what is bad or stressful – this can be really helpful; a simple change of mindset. It's a totally legitimate thought to say 'I have some leisure time but I'd like to have more'. Whereas what we actually tend to say is 'I have absolutely no leisure time!' which is rarely true. We then get caught up in a victim trap – because it's easier to do nothing about what we don't like in our lives than come at it from an 'action' point of view. Doing something about it takes energy and commitment.'

RECALL THREE GOOD THINGS

At the end of each day make a list of three good things that happened today. This can be anything from a good sandwich you ate to winning a client. The key is that you focus on the positive things, because when we do that, we start to look for them.

THE IMPORTANCE OF BEING IDLE

If busyness takes away our focus, then could it follow that idleness – doing nothing – improves it? Academics think so. This is because the 'space' given to us by doing nothing means we are able to think. Thinking is one of the key things that helps us to regain our thoughts and our focus, to literally 'reset the mind' to do what it really wants to do.

Tom Kreider[2] puts it like this:

'The space ... that idleness provides is a necessary condition for standing back from life ... making ... connections and waiting for the ... strikes of inspiration – it is, paradoxically, necessary to getting any work done.'

And not just any work done, but anything important to us done: the things we want to do with our families, our ambitions and dreams. ...

> **❝Without time to reflect ... we are doomed to live in purposeless and banal busyness.❞**
>
> Ben Hunnicutt, leisure researcher

ARE YOU EVEN AS BUSY AS YOU THINK YOU ARE?

Many psychologists and academics studying this so-called 'busyness' epidemic would argue you're not. For one, the numbers simply don't add up.

Sociologist John Robinson has been studying how people spend their time for decades. In 1997 he and Geoffrey Godby wrote *Time For Life* for which they analysed time diary data from 1965–85. What they found was surprising.

The time diaries (where people said where their time went) did not match people's actual time logs. People completely overstated how much they worked, and the more hours they claimed, the greater the discrepancy between their claim and the truth.

For example: People claiming to work between 50 and 54 hour weeks in their diaries overestimated by 9 hours, whereas people claiming to work 75 hour weeks, overestimated by 25. Robinson and his colleagues completed a similar study in 2011 and found exactly the same.

But hard data is not the only reason that Robinson – dubbed the 'Father of Time' – is generally cynical about how 'busy' we really are. He has plenty of anecdotal and academic research which suggests that people have a tendency to exaggerate how much they have to do and how little leisure time they have. Famously, Robinson asserts that his research proves that women, for example, have at least 30 hours leisure time per week (men have slightly more) if only they knew where to find it. And, crucially, weren't so busy being martyrs.

A wired, exhausted, overwhelmed Brigid Schulte nearly spat out her coffee when she heard about this elusive '30' hours. 'I don't know what you're talking about' she said. 'I don't have 30 hours of leisure time every week.' Keen to challenge Robinson's idea, she agreed to fill in what amounted to about six weeks' worth of time diaries so that Robinson could show her where this elusive leisure time was.

So how did Schulte's meeting with Father Time pan out? And what might it tell us about our perception of time and ultimately, how we spend it? Did he manage to find this elusive 30 hours of leisure time?

The main thing seems to be the discrepancy between what Schulte saw as leisure time and what Robinson saw.

BRIGID SCHULTE ON TESTING
ROBINSON'S *TIME FOR LIFE*

'I put it off for months. Part of me wanted to prove Robinson was wrong. Some days I felt so overwhelmed I could barely breathe. But honestly, I was more afraid than angry. What if Father Time was right? What if he found that I was squandering my time? What if I did have 30 hours of leisure and was simply too stressed out to notice? I kept my time diary in notebooks because my time didn't seem to fit into the 11 categories on the Excel spreadsheet he had given me. These included activities like "paid work", "sleep" "housework" and "leisure". But because I always seemed to be doing more than one thing at a time, I had to create my own category: "Doing Anything Else?"

In his office, Robinson took my notebooks, and began to hunt for leisure time. He highlighted every run, every 6 am DVD workout, every yoga class (leisure). Every time I read the newspaper he swiped it with the highlighter – even though I told him that was my job. "Reading is leisure" he said. He marked an hour when I was playing backgammon on the computer/arranged a cleaning service for my friend because her husband was battling cancer/visited a sick friend/talked to a friend about her leisure time while taking son's bike to the repair shop – all leisure. He even said that an hour waiting for the tow truck when my car had broken down would have been leisure, if I'd have been alone (I was with my daughter so it was considered childcare). I'd been afraid I not only had no leisure time, but that Robinson would find I didn't work enough. Instead we found I worked typically more than 50 hours a week, I slept an average of 6 hours a night. I spent almost every waking hour multi-tasking …

And my guilt that I wasn't spending enough time with the kids? One week I spent all but 7 hours in their presence. It wasn't all quality time, but I was there. I found I tidied in little scraps of time – which added to nearly an hour per day.

As a result of doing the time diary, I began to question everything I assumed was true about my life: that I didn't spend enough time with the kids, that I didn't work enough, that I needed to keep the house so tidy. Why did I feel it was my responsibility alone? Why did I feel I didn't deserve to relax until the to-do list was done? And what was the answer? I thought of the psychologist Erik Erikson, who said "The richest and fullest lives attempt to achieve an inner balance between three realms: work, love and play".'

It's clear that Robinson has some fairly fixed ideas about how we spend our time. He maintains that we 'exaggerate' our work hours to show how important we are. His studies also show that we sleep more than we think we do, watch too much telly and are not nearly as busy as we seem to feel.

'If we don't feel like we have leisure', he says 'it's entirely our fault. Time is a smokescreen. And it's a convenient excuse,' he told Schulte. 'Saying I don't have time is just another way of saying "I'd rather do something else."'

> ❝ **When you tell people they have 30–40 hours per week of free time they don't want to believe it.** ❞
>
> John Robinson, sociologist and Director of the Americans' Use of Time Project

The point – and the one we can take away from this – is: don't wait for leisure time, or special moments with your kids – take them whilst they're there. Just because a period of free time presents itself that you weren't expecting (getting locked out, the car breaking down) doesn't mean you can't put it to good use. Sometimes, all it takes is a simple change in mindset. Although this sounds simplistic and basic common sense, it's not always so easy to put into practice. How often have we chosen to feel defeated/irritated/inconvenienced by delays that could be seen as little windows of opportunity if we just flipped our mindset? How often have we said we 'don't have time' for exercise or to call a friend, without thinking what we could sacrifice (half an hour extra in bed for example) in order to make it happen? A big part of being focused is giving time to thinking how you *can* be; being creative and having a 'can do' mentality.

LAURA VANDERKAM ON CHALLENGING THE BUSY MYTH

Writer and speaker, Laura Vanderkam author of I Know How She Does It: How Successful Women Make the Most of their Time (for which she analysed 1001 days in working women's lives to try and find out …) is one such time researcher who doesn't buy this idea we are busier than we've ever been.

> *'I would definitely say we have more time than we think we do. I would also say that if you were a labourer in the 1880s and had to make your own furniture from scratch, didn't have a washing machine or were working in the fields all day – you'd be pretty busy! For my own research into how people (women) spend their time I looked at magazines from the 1950s (Fortune etc.) and they talk about how busy and hectic life was even then. So it's all relative. At all*

times, in all ages, people have believed that they couldn't possibly work any harder. But the great news is, that these days there is so much more choice on how you spend your time, and also so much support and information on how to do it well.'

Vanderkam's book is a challenge to this busy myth. She doesn't believe we're as busy as we say we are; she also believes, refreshingly, that we can have it all if having it all means the things that matter: family, community, love and leisure. She believes as we do that we absolutely have the power to shape our lives and that a full and meaningful life does not have to mean a stressful one.

HOW THE STORIES WE TELL OURSELVES KEEP US IN THE BUSY TRAP

It's human nature to tell ourselves stories about our lives. It's how we respond to challenges. Stories are comforting, that's why we love to hear them and tell them to young children. They have a structure: a beginning, middle and an end. The danger is that these stories are not always true – but we believe them.

Before Vanderkam wrote *I Know How She Does It*, she wrote another book called *168 Hours: You Have More Time Than You Think*. As a result she was asked to go into organizations and talk about how people could better spend their time. She would ask women to fill in half-hour by half-hour logs of what they did for an entire week and what she saw was interesting. When people actually wrote down their whole week's activities and events, they revealed that they had good, full, balanced lives, which involved time with their kids, husbands as well as leisure time.

It's human nature to concentrate on the stressful moments. After all, these are what make 'the headlines' as Vanderkam tells it. They're what make people laugh with recognition: 'I was so stressed, I left the house with odd shoes on', for example, or 'and then my client called but my toddler was screaming blue murder in the background'. However, if we were to sit down and tell the truth, we may be surprised: we may spend more time with our kids than we think we do, more time sleeping. More time having sweet moments.

And how did they do it? Again, it comes down to simple maths: there are 168 hours in a week. If you work 50 and sleep 8 per night (56 hours per week in total) that leaves 62 hours for other things. See? Perhaps you're not as busy as you think you are. Real focus means being truthful with yourself and not automatically believing the stories we tell ourselves that it's 'undoable' or 'all too much' (to learn how to make a time log, see Chapter 8).

“The time is there to 'have it all' if you know how.”

Laura Vanderkam, author and speaker

WE JUST *FEEL* BUSIER – THAT'S THE PROBLEM

Let's look at this concept of choice again. We have more than we ever had, about how to spend our time, what to focus our attention on, but could it be a blessing in disguise? Mark Forster is one person who thinks the increase in choices we have means we waste more time trying to make decisions and consequently feel overwhelmed. This, sociologists are calling 'decision fatigue', and it's a major focus robber.

MARK FORSTER ON THE PERILS OF TOO MUCH CHOICE

'It's not that we've got more work. It's that we've got so much more choice about what work to do/or what to do at any given moment. Because there could be a hundred different things we could be doing, and the more we rise up the executive ladder, the more choice we have.

If we go to a restaurant, we choose three things off that menu. But the trouble with life, is that we want to eat the whole menu; we fill our to-do list with all this STUFF, more stuff than we can ever eat, and there's nothing more overwhelming than having a back log, and feeling a lack of achievement. The average to-do list is 70–90 items long, and then we have to make a decision about what to do and what to do first, and making decisions actually depletes one's willpower (meaning we can't be bothered to do any of them).'

We're not denying that too much 'choice' can make our lives feel more complicated, but there is another way to look at it. What about if you found 'Real Focus' and could make this choice work for you; that the problem could be part of the solution? It's just working out how.

Sociologist Dalton Conley is known for his invention and coining of the word 'weisure' – meaning the blending of work and leisure. He does have things to say about weisure's drawbacks (the eroding of our private and public spaces for example – more of this later), but he also invites us to look at it in a 'cup half full' way. Having more choice over what we can do career-wise means that often our career becomes pleasure.

Many see '… the "rat-race" – work bleeding into our social lives and vice-versa – as a soul-crushing choice', he says. 'But the truth is, many people this day and age are doing work that they find rewarding and interesting. One of the great things about weisure, if we look on the upside, is that more and more people are and can, do jobs they are passionate about and so their work becomes pleasure.'

So there you are: just another way to look at it. Rather than seeing our feelings of being overwhelmed – of one thing blurring into the other – as a bad thing, perhaps we can look at it as a bonus or an opportunity. There is more than one way to look at 'focus' – it doesn't have to mean a structured, clean-cut life if that's not 'you'. It can also mean being wonderfully messy, as long as you're doing as much as possible of what you love and as little as possible of what you don't.

ASK YOURSELF

 When people ask how you are, do you frequently reply busy/manic/fried – delete as appropriate?

 How do you REALLY feel about your constant busyness? Do you genuinely enjoy your life like this or feel frequently overwhelmed?

 If it's the latter, what's stopping you changing things? (Identify three things; for example: fear of failure, the time to think about it, etc.)

 What, instinctively would you like to see more/less of in your life?

ARE YOU PRODUCTIVE OR JUST BUSY?

We are all at risk from the 'busyness' epidemic, as having a busy life has become synonymous with having a successful life. It can also be hard to say no when you have been brought up to equate hard work with success. But feeling overwhelmed undermines both your mental wellbeing and your ability to focus on what's important, especially if you have an inner dialogue telling you that you *should* be able to cope better. It's time to take a step back and look objectively at what's consuming the bulk of your time, and where you can make some changes.

Test by Sally Brown

QUESTION 1

A friend you haven't seen for a while asks how you are. You say:

A. I feel frazzled and exhausted
B. I'm busy, but OK
C. I've got a lot going on but it's all good

QUESTION 2

You notice a free weekend on the family calendar. You feel:

A. Not surprised. You plan regular free weekends to relax and be spontaneous
B. Pleased but slightly worried – there must be something you've forgotten?
C. Free weekends don't exist on my calendar

QUESTION 3

How do you usually tackle your to-do list?

A. I do a few easy tasks before tackling the tricky stuff
B. I focus on the most important tasks first
C. I'm lucky if I tick off one task a day, because other stuff always comes up

---

QUESTION 4

Which statement best describes your default mindset?

A. I'm so stressed out and have no time
B. My life is full and I love it
C. Life is hectic but I can just about cope

QUESTION 5

How do you feel about delegating your work and responsibilities?

A. It's easier to do it myself – I don't have time to give someone else the necessary instructions

B. I couldn't manage everything I do if I didn't delegate

C. I feel guilty as everyone else seems as busy as me

QUESTION 6

How often do you get a chance to think 'big picture' about your life?

A. About once a year, when I make my New Year's resolutions

B. I can't remember the last time

C. I make time to think about big plans and goals on a regular basis

QUESTION 7

You leave for a day out and realize you've left your smartphone at home. How do you feel?

A. Panic-stricken. I have to go back to get it

B. Irritated at the inconvenience and slightly distracted all day

C. Fine – it's not the end of the world

QUESTION 8

A work colleague asks what you did at the weekend. You:

A. Tell them about a film, theatre or music event you went to

B. Really struggle to think of what you did

C. Say you caught up on work and sleep

QUESTION 9

Which statement is closest to your typical evening?

A. Collapsing exhausted on the sofa when I've finally got everything done, then crawling into bed
B. I do some exercise, meet up with friends or spend time on my hobbies
C. Watching TV while trying to clear my emails or catch up on the work I haven't finished during the day

QUESTION 10

You meet a friend who talks about how hectic her life is. Do you:

A. Empathize – you're just as busy
B. Tell her you're even busier
C. Worry about her – it's not a healthy way to live

Now, add up your scores from each answer, and find out where you come on the following 'busy versus productive scale'.

	A	B	C
Q1	1	2	3
Q2	3	2	1
Q3	2	3	1
Q4	1	3	2
Q5	1	3	2
Q6	2	1	3
Q7	1	2	3
Q8	3	1	2
Q9	1	3	2
Q10	2	1	3

If you scored between 10 and 18…

You're drowning

You may have once thrived on busy, or seen it as a badge of honour, but now you feel like a hamster on a wheel. You're drained and exhausted but you've got so used to being busy that you feel guilty for relaxing or having time to yourself. You buzz through your days fuelled by adrenaline but now and then you crash, and pick up a bug that floors you (annoyingly, it often happens on holiday). You probably have a mental list of things you'd love to do 'when you have time'. But rather than fantasizing about a time in the future when you do things that bring you joy, how about introducing some into your life now?

If you scored between 19 and 24…

You're working hard to stay afloat

You're busier than ever these days but you're doing your best to hang onto your personal time and social life. The problem is you can find yourself sucked into taking on jobs and responsibilities that you resent. You're aware of when you feel frazzled and will then make a conscious effort to take on less and put your quality of life first. But 'busyness' can creep in and before you know it, you're frantic again. Your biggest frustration is that despite being so busy, at the end of each year, you never feel like your life's moved on. If you find it hard to say no, practise finding a 'soft no' that suits you, such as, 'I really can't say yes to that right now but do ask me again in the future.'

If you scored between 25 and 30…

You've found your equilibrium

You'd rather work smarter than harder, and see no merit in running around like a headless chicken. You're good at delegating and aim for good enough rather than perfect. You also value spontaneity, so try not to fill up every weekend with plans. You only wish more people shared your philosophy; our culture of 'competitive busyness' means it can be hard to stick to your principles at times. Reading a chapter or two of this book when you're wavering will remind you that you're on the right track.

CHAPTER 3

THE IMPACT OF BEING OVERWHELMED

S o we've established that we're all harried and unfocused (even if we're not, we feel it!). But why is it a problem? In this chapter, we explore what being in a state of constant busyness is doing to us; not only our minds but our bodies and the way we experience life. Above all, we'll explain how being forever caught up in the whirlwind of life actually stops us being able to carry out the cognitive processes that *allow* us to focus. When it comes down to it, it's a matter of physiology and the chemicals in our brains. But we don't have to be at the mercy of these chemicals, we can manipulate and control them if we know how and the first step is always awareness.

INFORMATION OVERLOAD

'Infobesity' – now there's a word you probably haven't heard of; but if you type 'Information Overload' into Wikipedia, it's the first word that comes up. It's a word that describes perfectly, perhaps, our very modern malaise. When we 'gorge' on information, we become unhealthy and out of shape, but it's not our waistlines that are suffering, it's our minds.

Of course even having the opportunity to 'gorge' on information is a very modern thing. The Information Age only exploded into our lives in the late nineties, early noughties; so the constant 'ping' of emails and notifications and texts and friend requests and tweets that interrupt our every waking moment (crazy when you think about it) is a relatively new phenomenon. All the research suggests, however, that it's already having a huge effect.

The main one being the effect it's having on our stress levels; this feeling (if we're to continue the 'obesity' analogy) of being overwhelmed by our lives that are too big, too over-flowing, too 'fat' with information and stuff.

Stress (and that little nasty hormone secreted when we are stressed: cortisol) can affect everything from our memories, to our immune systems, to our sleep. But did you know it actually makes our brains smaller (more of this later)?

Perhaps it's not surprising when we look at how much time we now spend 'gorging' on information online. For the average person that is 2 hours and 51 minutes per day.

The main reason for this is the rise of the smartphone, an entire computer in our pocket. Sixty-six per cent of adults now have one and we are so dependent on them, according to a survey carried out by Nokia, we can't go seven minutes without checking them. We do our shopping, banking and socializing on them, but also a lot of mindless 'looking'. The constant swipe to the left and scrolling on Twitter and Facebook is familiar with us all; it's almost like we don't know what to do with our fingers anymore without our device.

But what is this doing to us? In particular to our ability to have focus?

Nicholas Carr, author of *The Shallows: What the Internet is Doing to Our Brain* believes it to be a frightening amount. In fact, in a piece he wrote for the *Telegraph*[1] he went as far as to say 'the Net with its constant distractions and interruptions is turning us into scattered and superficial thinkers'.

But how? Carr, who wrote the book because he himself felt perpetually distracted, delved into studies to find out. In a nutshell he found that our constant exposure to the stimuli of the Information Age means our ability to 'pay attention' is shot. The problem is our brain can only make the neural connections necessary to solve the problems in our lives if we pay attention. But we can't pay attention because our attention is being constantly hijacked by the myriad distractions in our modern world:

> 'When we're constantly distracted and interrupted, as we tend to be when looking at the screens of our computers and mobile phones, our brains can't forge the strong and expansive neural connections that give distinctiveness and depth to our thinking. So our thoughts become disjointed, our memories weak.'[2]

So what happens then? We live on auto-pilot. Unable to focus enough to decide what truly matters in our lives, we almost sleepwalk through it, going about our business like a robot. You know the feeling: get up, school run, commute, run through emails, cook dinner, homework, keep head vaguely above water, repeat. Indeed, this is the very opposite to the Real Focus we seek.

Patricia Greenfield, a developmental psychologist, reviewed dozens of studies on how different media technologies influence our cognitive abilities. It wasn't all bad: she concluded that our growing use of screen-based media has strengthened visual–spatial intelligence, which can strengthen the ability to do jobs that involve keeping track of lots of rapidly changing signals, like piloting a plane or monitoring a patient during surgery. But since most of us won't be performing surgery or flying a plane any day soon, the weaknesses our Internet use cause are probably more important. These weaknesses tend to show up in what academics call the 'higher-order cognitive processes'. These include abstract vocabulary, mindfulness, reflection, inductive problem solving, critical thinking, and imagination.

All the things we need to focus and create lives we want to live.

'In a word,' says Carr 'we're becoming shallower.'

It's important to note here that not all distractions are bad. If we concentrate too long on a tough problem, we can get stuck in a mental rut, but if we walk away from the problem for a while, we often return to it with a fresh perspective. Research by the Dutch psychologist Ap Dijksterhuis indicates that these breaks in our attention give our unconscious mind time to grapple with a problem, meaning we then usually make better decisions. However, the constant distractedness that the Net encourages is very different from the kind of purposeful diversion of our mind that refreshes our thinking (walking/reading book).

ARE YOU ADDICTED TO DISTRACTION?

Perhaps all these distractions wouldn't be so bad if we were able to dip in and out of them – able to take or leave them – but research shows the opposite: that constant distraction creates a susceptibility to more distraction. So it becomes a case of supply creating demand.

Scientists at Stanford University found that individuals who spend a significant time online using social media were 'more susceptible to interference from irrelevant environmental stimuli and less able to concentrate on more than one task simultaneously'. This could be because when we get tweets or messages or any distractions the brain releases dopamine. Dopamine is the 'pleasure–reward' hormone – the same chemical that's released when we eat chocolate or smoke a cigarette or do anything 'addictive' – and it leaves us wanting more. In fact a 2012 study found that the brain treats Internet addiction similarly to drugs or alcohol; even anticipating those little electronic notifications has been found to trigger the release of dopamine in the brain, much like any craving and addiction.

How distractions affect life on a deeper level

So, in terms of finding Real Focus and ultimately managing our life better, what does this all mean? In short, it means that all our surfing and swiping and constant stimulation means we are not leaving any mental space for the things that really progress our lives. Things like contemplation, reflection and introspection. In fact, humans have become so obsessed with portable devices and overwhelmed by content that a study by Microsoft has found we now have attention spans shorter than that of a goldfish! (We have eight to their solid nine seconds, if you're interested.) When you consider that since 2007 that has fallen by four seconds, this is quite alarming!

DR TAMARA RUSSELL ON HOW TO STOP BEING DISTRACTED BY OUR PHONES

'We all get obsessed with answering and looking at our phones every 5 seconds – but why? Do we need to? Next time the phone rings or beeps, pause for a few seconds. Be aware it's made a noise but don't do anything. By slowing your immediate reaction to the phone (and the urge to engage with the device), you're gaining awareness.

By gaining awareness you can make a choice as to whether you need to look at it or if, actually, it can wait. You are training your mind to not react to distractions. The more you train and practise, the better you'll get. The mind is like plastic, it can mould and change.'

THE STRAIN ON OUR BRAINS

According to BUPA's 2013 stress survey, 44 per cent of Brits state they currently feel stressed and of them 27 per cent say they regularly feel close to breaking point. So we've established that our manic lives are stressing us out and that our addiction to information technology probably isn't helping matters. But what sort of effect is all this having on our actual brains? A lot, say scientists. In fact, it's shrinking them.

Emily Ansell and her colleagues from Yale Stress Center wanted to find out what is actually happening to the brain when someone is stressed out to the max, running around like a headless chicken. In order to do this they interviewed 100 otherwise healthy people to ascertain their stress levels, as well as doing a brain scan on each individual.

Those who had reported high levels of stress in their lives were found to have a pre-frontal cortex 20 per cent smaller in volume than those who hadn't. Pretty alarming! But what's so important about the pre-frontal cortex anyway? And how does this brain shrinkage actually affect our lives?

The pre-frontal cortex part of our brain controls our blood pressure and glucose levels, plus also what scientists call our 'executive functions'. These are things like how we think and reason, learn, plan, control our impulses and, most importantly, focus.

Basically, if we want to find Real Focus, we need our pre-frontal cortex to be in full working order. The trouble is, when we feel under pressure and stressed, our 'cave-man' survivalist side perceives a huge threat on the horizon (a mammoth, a spear coming our way) and our brains, including that ever-important pre-frontal cortex, are flooded with sugary, glucosey cortisol to give our bodies the energy needed to fight off the perceived 'threat'.

The pre-frontal cortex is also hugely important in that it also controls a little almond-shaped part of our brains called the 'amygdala' – otherwise known as the 'the seat of negativity' because it affects emotions such as aggression, fear, anxiety. When we're overwhelmed, the amygdala kicks into action – and we become emotional, angry and frustrated. The pre-frontal cortex tries to help you to cope and tell you it's all going to be ok, but because it's bathing in cortisol, it shuts down, making focusing almost impossible.

DR TAMARA RUSSELL ON THE 'RUMINATION VICIOUS CYCLE'

So why is feeling overwhelmed causing us to overthink?

'Information Overload is not just created externally. We create it within ourselves. This is because when we're stressed, often it's about uncertainty: in order to feel safer and get some certainty, we start thinking and simulating scenarios, that is we try to gain back control by ruminating about the past or obsessively pre-empting the future – both of which are futile. This thinking can arise out of anxiety, and the trouble is it uses up space in the brain which then can't be used for ordered, calm, strategic thinking; and it's the same space that we use to think about others. This is why when we are reacting to stress, it's harder to have empathy about others.'

So how might our hectic lives be affecting our relationships?

'Interpersonally we can become less sophisticated – we might snap at someone or say something we then regret because we haven't edited or inhibited our reactions in the way we can easily do when we are calm and relaxed. The simulation space of the mind we use to make inferences about what other people are thinking and feeling ('theory of mind' calculations) isn't working properly either because the pre-frontal cortex is in overdrive.'

It's for these reasons that we have far less capacity to be compassionate and giving to other people when we're overwhelmed and flooded with stress, and also why we try and (often wrongly) second guess what other people are thinking. But, as this chapter has shown, it's not just our personal relationships that suffer when we're constantly in 'fight or flight' response, it's every area of our lives: We lose the ability to focus, because we lose the ability to think clearly. 'Bathing in cortisol' as Schulte puts it, we are less able to plan, learn or control our impulses.

In short, our brains are so busy coping with the trauma of feeling out of control, that they have no space left for what matters. And, as we've touched upon, doing 'what matters' is really the crux of Real Focus and, ultimately, your happiness.

Sufficiently convinced and motivated to work on your focus? Then let's move on to Part Two, where we take a deeper look at the obstacles in your way and how we might overcome them.

66 Think about what you can do well, not how many things you can do. 99

Mark Forster, author and specialist in time management and organization

ASK YOURSELF

 On average, how much time do you spend online per day?

 How much time do you spend being 'idle' – just walking or sitting and thinking?

 How could you carve out more time to do this?

 How often do you check your smartphone?

 How could you reduce this, or be more mindful of your smartphone use?

HOW DISTRACTED ARE YOU?

Does your smartphone rule your life? If you can't imagine life without instant access to email and social media, you may be long overdue a digital detox. It's early days, but research is suggesting that responding to every notification could undermine your attention-span in the long term. In the short term, failing to set digital boundaries can be one of the biggest drains on focus and productivity. It's time to take an honest look at your clicking habits.

Test by Sally Brown

QUESTION 1

How often during the day do you check your phone?

A. Every time I get a notification, so every few minutes

B. I try to restrict it to every 15 or 20 minutes or so

C. I check it in the morning, at lunchtime and before I leave work

QUESTION 2

How much does work encroach on your leisure time?

A. I leave work behind at the end of the day and don't check my emails until I'm back at my desk

B. I reply to emails in the evening but don't really think of that as work

C. I always do some work in the evenings and at weekends because I can't get everything done during the day

QUESTION 3

How do you view social media?

A. I love it, and post to several sites on a daily basis

B. I use it to keep in touch with friends but only post now and then

C. I'm not signed up to any sites and happy that way

QUESTION 4

What best sums up your attitude to the information explosion of the past two decades?

A. It's great to have the world at your fingertips – most of the time

B. It's overwhelming – I can't keep up with all the articles, blogs and tweets

C. I dip into it as I need it

QUESTION 5

How long do you spend online in an average day (excluding time at work)?

A. More than two hours
B. Around an hour
C. Less than an hour

QUESTION 6

Your boss sends you an 'urgent' email just as you're about to have dinner with the family. You:

A. Answer it in the morning – my home life is precious and my boss knows I don't do emails in the evening
B. Answer it straight away – worrying about it would ruin my enjoyment of dinner anyway
C. Answer it when we've finished eating and apologize for the delay

---

QUESTION 7

How do you wind down on the way home from work?

A. I read a good book or listen to music
B. I work on the commute home, then relax with a glass of wine when I get in
C. With difficulty – I find it harder and harder to leave work behind these days

---

QUESTION 8

What do you do with your phone at bedtime?

A. Leave it charging downstairs
B. It's usually still in my handbag
C. Leave it by my bed – I check it last thing at night and first thing in the morning

---

Now, add up your scores from each answer, and find out your digital distraction score as follows.

	A	B	C
Q1	1	2	3
Q2	3	2	1
Q3	1	2	3
Q4	2	1	3
Q5	1	2	3
Q6	3	1	2
Q7	3	2	1
Q8	2	3	1

If you scored between 8 and 13...

You're in need of a digital detox

You've embraced new technology and are rarely far from a screen. You're active on social media, post several times a day, and do most of your social and professional communication online. Checking your phone is the first thing you do in the morning and the last thing you do at night. But you may now be wondering if you're addicted because you itch to check your phone every few minutes. You may also be conscious of setting a better example to your children. Start by turning the sound off your notifications – you have to have a will of iron to ignore the seductive 'ping' that signifies a new message. Try setting a timer while you work and don't check your mail or social sites until it goes off (start with ten minutes and work up to 40) and seriously consider a weekly digital detox – perhaps Sunday could become your screen-free day?

If you scored between 14 and 19...

You're struggling to protect your boundaries

You have a love-hate relationship with your smartphone – you love the convenience of having your emails and the internet on hand at all times, but the price you pay is never feeling you leave your work behind. You may also worry that your attention span is being eroded by your multi-tasking habit. Setting some boundaries on your digital life can help make room for neglected pleasures like reading, creative hobbies and face-to-face conversation. Try practising 'conscious computing' by introducing rules that work for you, such as no screens after 8pm in the evening.

If you scored between 20 and 24...

You're cyber-savvy

You're not immune to the lure of the digital world but you're wary of getting sucked in. You've resisted social media, partly to protect your privacy, but mainly because you prefer real friendships, not Facebook ones, and keep in touch via phone calls and texting. You've set clear boundaries at work and no-one expects you to reply to emails in the evening (although annoyingly, it doesn't stop them sending them). Your pet hate is friends who insist on having their phone on the table, picking it up to check every notification – could you find a polite way of letting them know?

2 WHY DO YOU LACK FOCUS?

CHAPTER 4

THE ATTENTION DEFICIT

e already touched on the Information Age and the subsequent 'crisis of attention' most of us find ourselves in, in Part One. In this chapter we're going to look at this in more depth, plus more reasons why we find it harder than ever to pay attention and how our focus is suffering. Most of all, we will give you ways to cultivate your focus: first by being aware of those constant distractions and second by avoiding their lure, so you can start to really reach your potential and get the most out of life.

EMAIL AND SOCIAL MEDIA

There's no denying that the emergence of email and social media has in many ways changed our lives for the better. We are more connected than we have ever been, we can communicate faster and more easily, and are only ever a couple of clicks away from the information we seek. However, as discussed in Part One, this 24/7 access to information and technology has, without a doubt, made us scatter-brained with the attention span of (less than) a goldfish! The constant pulls on our attention make it harder for us to make decisions and, ultimately, get things done.

Matthew Crawford, author of *The World Beyond Your Head: How to Flourish in an Age of Distraction*, says that in this technological age, we have allowed our lives 'to be colonized by the "hassle"'.

> **"Our distractibility indicates that we are agnostic on what is *worth* paying attention to. That is, what to value."**
>
> Matthew Crawford, academic and author

Email – whilst a fantastic tool when used correctly and something we couldn't imagine our lives without these days – is possibly the ultimate offender in terms of encouraging our minds to 'flit about' and causing our lives to feel fragmented. How many of us have been caught in the email black hole? That time-eating void that begins by breaking off from a task to attend to the 'ping' of a new email, only to emerge half a day later, having achieved nothing but a lot of email table-tennis, feeling exhausted and now unable to get back on task.

The trouble with email is that the more you respond to, the more you'll get. Then there's the chronic cc-ers to contend with who cc you in to each and every conversation to which you are often, only very tangentially, connected.

Entire days can be lost to clearing one's inbox if you're not careful, draining energy which could be used for 'real work'. So how do you keep on top of your inbox?

SIX GREAT WAYS TO GAIN CONTROL

1. *Canned responses:* Very often emails simply need a polite 'Sounds great, but I'll have to pass on this one' response, or a 'I need to think on this, I'll get back to you by the end of the week'. Most email systems have a tool to do this, meaning responses can be inserted into emails at the click of a button.

2. *Make everything in your inbox 'active' not 'reference':* What's the difference? Think of it like this: 'active' is anything you need to action (a client query for example), reference is something you've actioned already (an email relating to a meeting you've had, a

receipt of something) and which can therefore be filed away so as not to clog your inbox.

3. *Archive everything:* Create folders for everything: different projects, functions and/or areas of work, and personal stuff. Then get in the habit of putting emails in there as soon as you have replied to it or actioned it. You can also use the 'send and archive' tool which automatically stashes away your email once you're done with it.

4. *Create filters:* Spend some time adding filters, which can be created by doing a search and then clicking 'Create filter with this search', so that emails are sorted even before they hit your inbox. And add labels to conversations. This can be done automatically using filters so that they can be more easily retrieved via search at a later stage.

5. *Set up rules for incoming mail, helping to keep your inbox clear:* You can either choose to automatically forward the mail, move it to a specific folder, or send straight to trash. To set up rules, click 'Message, 'add rules'. Set your email software to 'receive' messages only at certain times, so that you're not distracted by incoming messages.

6. *Set aside time to read and respond to email:* After a period of really focus-heavy work, or at the time of day when your energy and creativity are at their lowest. Explain to colleagues that you only check email at certain times, and that they can call you if the matter is really urgent.

MARK FORSTER ON 'INBOX ZERO'

What is it?

'I recommend and use myself, an "inbox zero" approach to all my work. What this means is that you finish all your current work, whilst keeping

- Your inbox of new mail empty.
- Your inbox of new paper empty.
- Your inbox of new tasks empty.'

Why use it?

'You keep your active projects fully up to date, not taking anything new on until they are completed. This is the only sensible way to work because each new day brings new tasks, so if you haven't got rid of the new tasks from one day by the time you start the next day, when are you going to do them? People say, "when I have more time" – but when is that going to be?'

If you can't maintain the Inbox Zero approach, what does this tell you?

'If you find that you can't keep up with an inbox zero approach to your work, then you can take that as a sign that you have more work than you are capable of coping with. People say things like, "I'd never be able to keep up with clearing everything straight away" – but if you can't remain on top of things today, when exactly will you be able to?'

And what's the solution?

'Not to stress yourself out by ramping up your efforts, but taking a realistic look at what you're trying to achieve in life and then throw everything out that's not part of that vision.'

Nobody's suggesting that an 'inbox zero' policy is the only way to keep control of your emails – it's just one way. It may be that you find that no more than 50 emails in your inbox at one time is a more realistic and achievable number. The most important thing is that you find a system (see Chapter 10 for more on the importance of systems) that works for you.

And when we say 'work' we mean that it stops you thinking about your inbox so you can get on with what really needs to get done. Remember the glass jar theory from Chapter 2? Emails are the sand that can and should fit around the big stuff, not the other way around. And this will happen more easily if you have a good email system. There's nothing more distracting from the task in hand, after all, than the 'chatter' in your head from the 50 or more emails in your inbox that need dealing with, or 'new email!' accompanied by that maddening ping, flashing up In the corner of your screen every two minutes whilst you're trying to do something else. Nobody can focus with those sorts of distractions.

Ever heard of the saying 'Look after the big stuff and the small stuff will take care of itself'? Well, we could take the opposite view when it comes to email: take care of this bitty, small stuff and you'll be able to focus on the big stuff a lot more easily.

PROCRASTINATION AND PRIORITIZATION

A huge part of our 'crisis of attention', as Matthew Crawford dubs it, is our difficulty with *what* to pay attention to. Due to the avalanche of choices these days about what to focus on, be that social media, email, the news channel running 24/7 across our screens, we don't know what to choose, or what we value most anymore.

We then waste a lot of time trying to make decisions about this, and decision-making is a very exhausting, energy-sapping pursuit. So we have a vicious cycle:

Too much choice

= attention deficit or crisis of attention

= using up lots of energy trying to make decisions

= not much energy left to focus in the first place.

So what happens then? We procrastinate. It seems like we have so much to do that we don't know where to start – so we become paralysed and don't do anything – it's a big reason for our focus to falter.

How does procrastination affect our ability to focus?

We all put things off from time to time, but if you procrastinate as a matter of habit, it can have a devastating effect on your career, your personal relationships and your life in general. This is because, by constantly putting things off, you severely limit your levels of achievement and constantly fail at what should be the moment of fulfillment – for example getting tickets to a show or an interview for a job. Even if it affects small things – like catching the train we need to get – if we fail often enough it can really affect our self-esteem and therefore our focus. What's the point in striving, we then think, if I never achieve anything I set out to do? And there are our stress levels to think about: the pressure that comes from knowing you are nearing a deadline but haven't started the work, or missing a deadline and STILL having to do it, can be enormous. It makes you wonder why on earth we continue to put things off.

Researchers in procrastination at Carleton University in Canada did an online survey. They received 2700 replies to the question: 'To what extent is procrastination having a negative effect on your happiness?' Forty-six per cent said 'quite a bit' or 'very much'.

Why do people procrastinate?

So why *do* we? When all the evidence tells us that it doesn't do us any good? Understanding this may help us to address our behaviour.

According to academics, procrastination often begins in early adolescence (age 9 to 13) when we learn that a good tactic for gaining control over our parents is putting off things they want us to do – whether that be homework, chores or family obligations. We are guilty of both delay (putting off until tomorrow) and denial (telling ourselves that tomorrow will never come). The problem is, whilst the instant gratification is relief at not having to do the thing we don't want to do, this causes a lot more stress in the long term when the deadline gets nearer and the pressure gets greater. We then enter head-spin mode and can't focus on anything!

How do people procrastinate?

According to psychologists, there are many different types of procrastination but the two most common are:

1. **Behavioural procrastination**

   This tends to be a self-sabotage strategy, where you use procrastination as an excuse. For example, you may do badly in an exam but then blame it on procrastination (you didn't get round to revising) rather than your own abilities.

The psychologist Joseph Ferrari, Professor of Psychology at DePaul University in Chicago, also thinks that procrastinators suffer from self-doubt and worry about how other people judge their abilities. 'Procrastinators view their self-worth as based on ability,' he says. 'So their logic goes, "If I never finish the task, you can never judge my ability".'

2. **Decisional procrastination**

The decisional procrastination strategy is to put off making a decision when dealing with conflicts or choices. People who do this tend to be afraid of making a mistake and are likely to be perfectionists. They tend to seek out more and more information before attempting to make a decision (if they make one at all) and then reach a stage of 'optional paralysis': they've created so many choices for themselves that they feel unable to choose for fear of choosing an option that is less than perfect.

How can I overcome procrastination?

The good news is that there are many ways – none of them, by the way, to do with time management. Ferrari says, 'It's not about time management. To tell a chronic procrastinator to "Just Do It" is like telling a clinically depressed person to cheer up.'

A big move towards overcoming procrastination is prioritization, and there are several ways we can learn to do this better and more effectively.

Pareto Analysis is a simple technique for prioritizing problem-solving work so that the first piece of work you do resolves the greatest number of problems. It's based on the Pareto Principle (also known as the 80/20 Rule) – the idea that 80 per cent of problems may be caused by as few as 20 per cent of causes. You can do this on your own, but this is a particularly great way of working as a team to prioritize tasks, making everybody feel like they've had an input.

How to apply the Pareto Analysis technique

- Identify a list of problems and their causes.

- Then score each one according to the type of problem you're trying to solve. So, for example, if you're trying to increase profit you might score each problem on how much it's costing the company.

- Next, group the problems together by their cause (need to speak to client, not enough training).

- Then, add up the score for each group of problems.

- Finally, work on finding a solution to the cause of the problems in the group with the highest score – that group is your priority task.

When inheriting or being suddenly faced with a multitude of problems (say if you were to suddenly be made Head of Department or Chair of a Committee) the Pareto Principle can be very useful in helping you to identify and focus on the most important problem, which, when solved, will generate the most significant improvements to the overall situation.

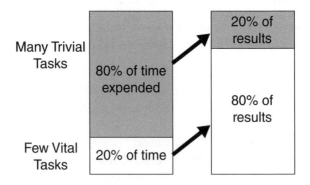

The Pareto principle

! SWITCH FROM HIGH- AND
   LOW-ATTENTION TASKS TO
   GIVE YOUR BRAIN A BREAK

A 'high-attention' task would be something that requires more concentration, such as writing a report. A 'low-attention' task would be something that you don't need to think too much about, such as filing.

If we work like this, we work far more efficiently and can go for longer than if we:

1. **Multi-task** – that is, try to do several things at once. This just means that we fail to reach 'flow' in any activity and end up doing many things badly rather than one thing well.

2. **Spend too long doing a 'high-attention' task**. This basically results in the brain burning a lot of glucose, fast, leaving us feeling depleted and unable to continue with the high-attention task as long as if we broke it up with low-attention tasks which enable the brain to rest. Think of it like interval training: a short burst of high-intensity exercise such as sprinting, followed by walking, repeated several times, is much more efficient for the body than attempting to sprint for a long time.

MARK FORSTER'S TIPS FOR
OVERCOMING PROCRASTINATION AND
MAKING DECISIONS

- 'If you are feeling overwhelmed by what to pay attention to, it's usually because you have bitten off more than you can chew. Rather than asking yourself what to

> do first, ask yourself should you be doing it at all?
> (Remember: say no at commitment level if possible,
> rather than once you've agreed to the task, otherwise
> you are failing in your commitments.)
>
> * Rather than write a long list of low, medium and high
>   priority, it's more effective to limit the number of things
>   in each category. For example you might say you
>   can have ten things in medium, but only five in high
>   priority.
>
> * Remember there are no right or wrong decisions, only
>   decisions with different consequences. You need to train
>   yourself to stop looking for the perfect decision. Instead,
>   your attitude needs to be that you take decisions and
>   deal with the consequences. Start with small decisions
>   first – like what email will I reply to first? What will I have
>   for tea? The fact that you could flip a coin to make these
>   decisions takes the pressure off and, the more you do it,
>   the more confident you become in making choices and
>   decisions.'

When we have a to-do list as long as our arm it can feel overwhelming. We are faced with something that feels too big for us – hence we procrastinate. We hope you can see, however, how constant procrastination can, if left unchecked, have devastating effects on our sense of self-worth and our progress in life in general. As we've outlined, learning to prioritize is helpful because it helps us chunk things up into bite-size portions rather than wrestle with the daunting big picture. In the coming chapters there will be many more tips and ways you can confront procrastination and other symptoms of being overwhelmed, and move instead towards Real Focus.

WEISURE

Weisure: The blending of work and leisure – a word coined by American sociologist, Dalton Conley – could be another offender where loss of your focus is concerned.

So, imagining you've got a hold on your emails, you then have to contend with the lure of social media. And it's not just the constant pings and notifications, or even the dopamine hits (as discussed in Part One) that we get every time we refresh our Facebook or Twitter page that cause us to be unfocused. It goes deeper than that. We are distracted on an emotional level. Consider, for example, that you get a Facebook notification – someone has commented on your post and you can't resist seeing what they've said, but then, once on Facebook, you see that so-and-so has just got engaged/bought a new amazing house/ just run a 10k in record time. You suddenly feel a bit deflated and inadequate. You suddenly feel, ironically, like that person who wastes time on social media when you could be achieving worthwhile things.

Facebook and social media affect our confidence and our mood because they encourage us to compare ourselves to other people; providing a window into our peers' lives that we don't always want but meaning they are paraded in front of us whether we like it or not. This can be far more distracting than just those pings!

American sociologist Dalton Conley believes that the transparency of people's lives that social media allows and the blurring of our public and private lives (colleagues being our Facebook friends; friends very often being our colleagues) is causing us to feel overwhelmed. This is because we are more exposed and can't retreat into our private sphere – or as Conley calls it, into our 'backstage selves'. Add to that the pressure that comes with our every failure and achievement being on show for all to judge, and it's not surprising we're so distracted.

Indeed, 20 years ago, we wouldn't have known that our friend got a swanky new job, or was in the Caribbean, so we would have no need to be distracted for the rest of our day while we stew in life envy!

'With social media we see the vast chasm above and below of what people are achieving', says Conley. 'The space between the ones who are getting ahead and who are not. If you are not keeping up in your job you can see there's a long way to fall for you and your kids if you don't keep up.'

Dalton Conley – as well as writing many best-selling books about our modern lives including *Elsewhere USA* ('Elsewhere' being 'the constant state of motion and distraction that takes you anywhere and everywhere but here') – is also famous for coining the word 'weisure': the blending and blurring of work and leisure.

DALTON CONLEY ON WEISURE

'Increasingly, it's not clear what constitutes work and what constitutes fun, be it in an office or out in the street. We're using smartphones to do business while out with our families or chatting with Facebook friends while having a conference call. Whereas 20 years ago, you'd maybe come home with some paperwork, now you can operate an entire business on your Android so there's never any reason NOT to be available to your boss or your clients.

How is weisure contributing to our feelings of being overwhelmed?

It's a perfect storm of technology and economics. Because we can work all the time, because of smartphones and wi-fi, we feel we should. We really are connected all the time and we feel increasingly like if we don't do all the work all the time, then we'll fall behind, so we feel overwhelmed and pressured. You could go and live in a yurt and live a totally disconnected life but, economically, you know you wouldn't keep up. Those who can master technological advancements will get ahead of us, it's plain and simple.

There's also the fact we never switch off

If you can get an email at 1 am or you're replying to emails on your commute to and from work instead of decompressing, you begin to feel exhausted and overwhelmed. It requires a great deal of discipline to resist the urge to work in the technological age. It's ironic that relaxing takes a huge force of will.

Are there upsides to weisure?

More and more people are doing jobs they love (which they're also passionate about). This means their work becomes pleasure and for an increasing number of people is a source of meaning and fun, rather than just a means of paying the bills. Basically, our work hours are longer but our enjoyment of work is more.'

So, could weisure – the blending of work and leisure – actually be a good thing if you know how to make it work in your favour? And how might you do this?

Well, it obviously depends on the individual; some people like to mix work with pleasure more than others, after all, and as we've said, for some lucky people work is pleasure. In general, though, the following are good guidelines for being a 'weisure' aficionado rather than letting it get the better of you:

- If you're going to mix work and leisure, set your own boundaries to ensure you don't become too overwhelmed and distracted: for example, don't look at your phone after a certain time in the evening or don't be 'friends' with bosses or anyone senior to you on Facebook. After all, you don't need your boss knowing you've been hungover all day at work!

- If you are going to do more work when you get home, at least allow some 'decompression' time on your commute or journey home, or even in your lunch hour. Carve out little pockets of complete leisure time within your work time (a walk at lunchtime/even popping in to see an exhibition/only reading novels not reports on the train home). That way, you'll keep your batteries burning longer because you'll constantly be recharging yourself. Remember, there's nothing more un-relaxing than trying to relax while doing other things – it only leads to that awful, nagging 'I'm on holiday so why do I feel like I left the cooker on at home?' feeling.

Above all and as far as possible – do what you love. Then it won't feel like work at all.

REAL PEOPLE
"How I dealt with my addiction to social media"
– *Laura*

'Because I work from home, there is always the strong temptation to waste time on the Internet and social media. With nobody there to enforce boundaries around using Facebook and Twitter, I could easily find myself getting sucked in. It was a vicious circle and totally distracting – I'd find myself on Facebook, sometimes for hours, only to come off it feeling ashamed like I'd just been in the pub for hours! These feelings of shame would then make it even harder to focus: "I've just wasted a whole morning – I may as well go the whole hog", was my thinking. Or I'd have got so sucked into whatever trivial thing we were discussing on Twitter that I couldn't bring my focus back to the work task in hand.

I was also finding that spending time on Facebook or Twitter could ruin my day. I began to compare my life to others' or find myself replying to one person, then "coming up for air" half an hour later having been looking at the photographs of someone I hadn't seen since school. A friend of mine described working like being "on fire" and social media being like the bucket of water that you want to jump into, and this is exactly how it felt. I was doing it as a way of avoiding doing really hard work which required me to really focus and use my brain.

In the end, I got so sick of myself, I deactivated my Facebook and Twitter account. It made the world of difference. I didn't waste so much time anymore and consequently got so much more done and felt better about myself. Once it had gone from my life, I didn't miss it either. It made me realize there was nothing to miss! I didn't need to know what was happening in everyone else's lives, I needed to concentrate on my own.

These days, I am on Facebook and Twitter (turns out, slightly annoyingly, it's very easy to "reactivate" your account). However, I manage myself a lot better and whenever I feel my concentration dipping and my productivity waning, I go on a little Social Media Boycott. Friends are used to it now and the real ones just email me if they need to contact me. It always sorts my head out.'

In this chapter – The Attention Deficit – we have explored, in more depth, the things that make claims on our attention and stop us from focusing. We hope you feel, at least, like you are far from alone. We live in a very distracting world, constantly bombarded by these focus robbers (see more about focus robbers in Chapter 6). However, we hope you've been able to take away strategies to help you cultivate your focus and understood that a lot of Real Focus is merely deciding *what* to pay attention to – or, put in another way, what you feel deserves most of your attention.

ASK YOURSELF

 What system do you have in place (if any) for checking your email? For example, at what time of day and how often? What measures could you take to make email less distracting for you?

 How often do you check your Facebook account? How does it (honestly) make you feel when you do? Keep a 'Facebook Diary' for a week to monitor its effects on your mood and your focus.

 Do you have clear boundaries between 'work' time and 'home time'? If not, how could you make them clearer so that you can reclaim some of the 'backstage' you? For example, have a time beyond which you don't check work emails.

DO YOU KNOW HOW TO PRIORITIZE?

Do you ever wonder if the main thing sabotaging your focus is *you*? Everyone procrastinates in one way or another, and it's wrong to simply dismiss it as laziness, as some forms of procrastination are part of creative thinking. It's also easy to lose sight of your priorities, or to stay in your comfort zone and use up your time on the easy stuff. But sometimes, just a small shift in the way you approach the challenges ahead can make a big difference. Take our test to find out how good you are at prioritizing, and where you need to make some changes.

Test by Sally Brown

QUESTION 1

What comes to mind when you're faced with a task and feeling overwhelmed?

A. Do I really need to be doing this, and if so, who can help me?

B. I'll think about it later

C. I'm so stressed. I'll never get this finished

QUESTION 2

Which description best fits your email inbox?

A. Semi-organized chaos. I clear it on a regular basis but it's amazing how quickly it builds up

B. Complete chaos. I have so many unread emails it's embarrassing

C. Inbox zero. I read then delete, action or archive all new emails at the end of each day

---

QUESTION 3

Which statement do you most agree with?

A. I feel more distracted these days than ever before

B. I've made a conscious effort to minimize distractions

C. I have distracted days but days when I can focus

QUESTION 4

In the last few minutes, you have:

A. Completely focused on doing this test

B. Done the test while also thinking about what I need to do afterwards

C. Kept mainly focused on the test with a bit of daydreaming

QUESTION 5

You have a lunch date with a friend. Who is the most likely to have arranged it?

A. The friend – if it's left to me, things never happen
B. It varies – if I've got time I do the organizing, but if I'm busy, my social life falls off my agenda
C. Me – I'm always the one who pins people down to dates

QUESTION 6

You need to make a big decision within seven days. When do you make it?

A. Straight away, otherwise it hangs over me and distracts me
B. Just before the deadline – urgency helps me focus
C. After the deadline, when someone prompts me

QUESTION 7

You have a meetings-free day in the office – how do you decide what task or project to focus on?

A. There's no plan – I answer emails and sort out problems as they come up
B. I make an early start on my most urgent project while I'm fresh, then do some forward planning
C. I start with some easy tasks and try to get on to important stuff by the end of the day

---

QUESTION 8

Your train is delayed by 15 minutes. How do you use the time?

A. I get a cup of tea then sit and daydream or call a friend for a chat
B. I answer work emails on my phone
C. I flick through the free paper or scroll through Facebook

Now, add up your scores from each answer, and find out how prone you are to procrastination as follows.

	A	B	C
Q1	3	2	1
Q2	2	1	3
Q3	1	3	2
Q4	3	1	2
Q5	1	2	3
Q6	3	2	1
Q7	1	3	2
Q8	3	2	1

If you scored between 8 and 13...

You're a pro at procrastination

You've got into the habit of mentally parking future plans and projects for 'when you have time', which never happens, so your days tend to be spent in reactive rather than proactive mode. You may have perfectionist tendencies, and want to make the 'best' decision, or hold off tackling a project until you feel in the 'right' frame of mind. But any decision or action is better than inaction, so try aiming for good enough instead of perfect. It may surprise you that the main impact in your 'drop' in standards is appreciation from friends and colleagues – procrastination can be deeply frustrating for those left waiting for you to respond.

If you scored between 14 and 19...

You're a periodical procrastinator

You know you feel better when you don't procrastinate, but there are times when you feel so overwhelmed and exhausted that you don't have the mental headspace to give decisions the focus they need. You have more productive periods when you catch up, but it's an unhelpful pattern, as your periods of procrastination can erode both your confidence and your mood. Getting enough sleep is important, as nothing undermines focus and motivation like tiredness. You may also want to rethink your to-do list – it can be tempting to tackle the easiest tasks, so only write down what's really important.

If you scored between 20 and 24...

You're proactive

You've learned from experience that the most productive way to work is by biting the bullet and tackling the trickiest or most important tasks of the day first, no matter how tempting it may be to put it off. You're realistic about what you can achieve in a day so you don't make long to-do lists, preferring to focus on one or two key tasks. People are in awe of your motivation but you also have days when you feel a bit 'blah' about your work. Your secret is that you get started anyway, because you know that motivation follows action. You can get frustrated with the procrastinators in your life, but could you show some compassion and encouragement instead?

CHAPTER 5

FINDING A BALANCE: MEN, WOMEN AND OUR CHANGING ROLES

A big aspect of achieving Real Focus in your life depends on the people around you. None of us is an island. Whether we like it or not, we exist as part of families and workforces; we exist as part of society. Finding Real Focus in our lives means doing so in a way that is in harmony with the people around us. Yes, you're seeking to live 'your life', 'your way', but that's no good if it's to hell with everyone else! Your life includes the people who matter, and part of finding Real Focus means working with them, not against them. In order for that overwhelmed feeling to lift and serenity to prevail (imagine!), our life-load needs to feel like it's shared fairly, and it helps to feel clear about our roles.

It's for this reason that we couldn't write a book about finding Real Focus without talking about the gender divide – the impact and expectations of our roles, as defined or dictated by society, culture as well as the opposite sex. And of course, most importantly, how all this affects our ability to focus.

THE SO-CALLED GENDER REVOLUTION

In terms of the roles we play and are expected to play, it seems both men and women are confused. We aren't clear what our roles or our responsibilities are anymore, and it's causing our focus to waver, and many of us – women and men – to feel conflicted, resentful and, ultimately, overwhelmed. We all want to have a 'balanced life' and it seems so simple when we say it like that, but achieving it seems to be another thing entirely.

In an article in *The Observer* (3 August 2008) entitled 'Are Men The New Women?', which is essentially about men's confusion over their identity, Rosie Boycott has an interesting argument. Boycott, who launched *Spare Rib*, a feminist magazine in the seventies, argues that gender equality shouldn't just mean women having more 'work/life balance' while the men have all the financial responsibility. Rather, it should mean liberation for *both* sexes. She makes the point that a man being solely financially responsible for his children *and* his wife and only having two weeks holiday a year, can feel as trapping as a woman who is responsible for all the childcare and the housework. Neither is 'work/life balance'.

There is also the fact, she points out, that there's still a way to go for society (i.e. bosses, mainly) to fully accept men taking time out from their day at work, to take their child to the dentist or doctor for example. This, in turn, means that many men feel uncomfortable doing it, or even asking to do it, and until that changes there is not real 'equality'.

Whether you agree with that is another matter. But going back to our point that Real Focus, if it were to be boiled down to its core, is really about 'doing what matters', what Boycott says helps us see how this can get lost when the structures of life and the roles society carves out for us don't allow it; and it's clear both men *and* women feel disgruntled when this happens.

Obviously everybody is different and has their own set of circumstances to contend with in terms of finding balance and focus in their lives. However, sociologists and psychologists have pinpointed a few reasons why balance and gender equality remain elusive for so many of us. Perhaps it's important to note that things aren't helped along by facts such as that men in the UK have the most unequal paternity rights in Europe, and women still earn 12 per cent less than men.

THE STALLED GENDER REVOLUTION

One of the main issues is that the improvement in equality between the sexes that began in the sixties, kind of ... stalled. The sixties were seen as a huge milestone in gender equality – the invention of the contraceptive pill meant that women could choose when they had a family or even if they did, and this had a huge bearing on their earning potential and career choices. Things progressed; more women went out to work than ever before in the late seventies and early eighties, but then the 'second shift' was born. The sociologist Arlie Hochschild first wrote about the second shift in the eighties – about how women come home from a full day of work to a 'second shift' of housework and childcare – but the same is true now. Even though time studies show men are doing more around the house and with the kids, women are still doing twice as much. Sociologists call it the 'stalled gender revolution'.

There are many reasons for this phenomenon; among them the fact that women have had incentives to go into 'male' jobs but not the other way around; also the simple fact that there are centuries of gender stereotyping to get over. The worst hit seem to be working mums, however (the trouble starting when the first baby comes along). Before that, the division of chores and the ability to work is equal and then … everything changes for the woman but not so much for the man.

This is because this country has unfortunately not yet found a way for it to work for the majority of working mums. Childcare is so expensive that it doesn't make sense for a lot of women to go to work – or at least to be able to do the same hours and offer the same level of commitment. This creates the 'second shift syndrome' where women are doing a three- or four-day week, but still coming home to bathe the kids, cook the dinner and do homework. It's also usually the part-time working parent who has to take time off when their child is sick, or it snows and the school shuts down.

Even when there are situations where the woman is the breadwinner, the domestic chores are often down to them because of what? It's hard to tell: long-held cultural assumptions about gender, because women tend to have higher standards, who knows? But the evidence of an ever-wide gender gap is there.

In 2014 a survey by Mumsnet found that women do twice as much housework as men, even when they've done a full day in the office. It's no wonder women feel like they can't focus on what's important – because for many of them, everything seems like it is.

Justine Roberts, Chief Exec of Mumsnet said: 'One in three working mums is the main family wage earner – a rise of 1 million over the last 18 years. Despite this, women are still busting a gut back home, responsible for the vast majority of chores. It's not surprising we talk about glass ceiling and the lack of women at the top. Most of us are just too exhausted to climb the greasy pole.'

REAL PEOPLE

"How I created healthy boundaries between work and leisure" –Richard

'My dad used to work stupid hours from an early age and he was never around. I always knew I didn't want to be a Dad like that – I wanted to be around for my kids. Lizzie, my wife, and I decided before our first son was born in 2004 that we both wanted to work part time. I've never been an alpha male, career-driven type and Lizzie's not a stereotypically girl-girl – we've always been in the middle in terms of roles even before we were married and had kids, so to some extent how we've made it work so equally was our destiny.

I had a good relationship with my boss and he was very supportive when I explained to him in no uncertain terms that this was what was important to me. I think, especially as a man, you have to be very upfront about it if you want to go part-time and you have to expect ramifications career-wise. I got promoted – but then my boss brought also someone in above my head. My nose was pushed out of joint to a certain extent but then I did think fair enough – I realized you can't have your cake and eat it.

Having boundaries around work and personal time is really important to me and I am pretty strict about it. I have my day off on Thursdays and unless there is something really important, I make it understood that to take any work calls or emails would be beyond the call of duty. I always clear my inbox on the way home on a Wednesday night and don't do emails at home.

There are two reactions to me working part time: people with kids who look at me with envy and jealousy; people without kids, who are young and hungry for it, and can't understand why I wouldn't want to work all the hours possible. I make it known though that I get paid less! That's the trade-off.

On my day off, I take the kids to school and pick them up. I really appreciate that time with them. Domestically, my wife and I try to split things down the middle at home. It's the handover that's sometimes difficult – one going to work and telling the other that so and so needs a bottle to take for the tombola, or it's "wear something red" day. You have to really communicate, and we also synch our calendars on our phone so we know what the other's doing.

My day off is generally a recovery day. I go for a run, do a few jobs around the house and do things like plan an expedition or camping trips with the kids. I do worry that

I'm not where I should be on the career ladder, but I always wanted to be there for the kids when they were young. There's something about putting a boundary around work and having that extra day that makes it feel real, like I've accomplished doing what's really important to me. I feel like I'll look back and be glad we're making it work.'

THE SEXIST SHIFT

Research has found that social attitudes of men become significantly more conservative after the birth of their first child. Before children, most men believe that the chores should be divided equally, but fatherhood seems to bring about a 'sexist shift' in many men, who take the opinion that women should do the lion's share of the housework and childcare.

The study, carried out by a team of researchers at The University of Queensland in Australia and the Goethe University Frankfurt in Germany, surveyed almost 1800 people before and after the birth of their first child. They were asked to express how strongly they agreed with various statements, using a scale of 1 to 7 – where 1 signified 'strong agreement' and 7 signified 'strong disagreement'. The statements covered such issues as breadwinning, social barriers and maternity leave.

When asked if women alone should undertake the stereotypically female roles of housekeeping and care of the children, men were notably more supportive of this statement, believing that the household burden should not be equally shared across the sexes.

Even more pronounced was the change in reaction to the statement that 'a working mother can establish just as good a relationship with her children as a mother who does not work for pay'. After birth, women were 4 per cent more likely to support the idea, while men fell by an average of 0.1 per cent.

'When their first child is born, men and women grow more traditional in their gender attitudes towards mothering, as well as about who does housework and caregiving', says one of the study authors Janeen Baxter. She calls this the 'sexist shift'.

However, just because men agree that women should do most of the domestic chores in a survey, does not mean they feel entirely comfortable with this. It seems that the confusion about roles and gender imbalance is not just limited to women – men too are feeling at sea, not sure of what their role is. Some academics, such as Kathleen Parker, author of *Save the Males*, believe this is because men are receiving conflicting messages from women but also society as a whole. On the one hand we want them to be providers and protectors – except when we don't. Women are sometimes guilty of wanting men to be there to see the birth and do the midnight feeds, but then won't let them do much else, because it's not being done 'their way'.

> **❝All this confusion is causing us to feel more overwhelmed and unsure of our place in life.❞**
>
> Brigid Schulte, author of *Overwhelmed*

ROLE-SHIFTING AND ROLE OVERLOAD

We've talked about multi-tasking and the negative effects that can have on our ability to focus in earlier chapters, but the 'multi' does not just refer to 'tasks' – it also refers to roles. More than ever, men and women are what psychologists call 'role shifting'. They go from parents to workers, back to parents again. Or they feel they have to be good sons and daughters, friends, employees and general super-humans. Whereas perhaps 40 years ago it was the cultural norm for your life to be made up of 'work' and 'family' commitments, now there is more pressure – certainly with the arrival of social media where we're all 'on show' – to also throw great parties, do good work for charity and push ourselves with physical challenges (triathlon, anyone?). Flexibility and variation in life are great, but if you feel you have to be all things to all people, it's stressful. And these gear-shifts and role shifts are exhausting, because everything requires attention, and yet we can't give the same attention to everything.

Once upon a time, 'having it all' for a man probably meant climbing up the corporate ladder, a wife at home who looked after the kids, money, nice holidays etc. But – contrary to Baxter's study (nothing ever being black and white after all!) – other studies are showing men want to have a meaningful career and a rich family life and are finding out just how hard it is. The days of them having one role – 'provider' – are over, but where does that leave them? What is a modern man's role these days? Many men are confused and unsure about this and it's leading to lack of focus.

REAL PEOPLE
"How we carved out roles that worked for us" – *Sarah*

'I was working full time in a full-on, client-facing role for a management consultancy firm when I had my daughter, Anya. I decided I wanted to go back to work full time

---

because I enjoy it. However, I wanted to work at home one day a week; but the organization I was working for at the time said no – it was at that point I knew something had to change and decided to change jobs. But instead of downgrading, I decided to upgrade. I decided to go for the money so that my husband Harry and I might have more choices in the future.

The company I got a job with (another management company) was even more full on than the last – the sort that prides itself on counting on employees who can be there at the drop of a hat, 24/7. They'd have you working 12–14 hour days if you let them. It's a very competitive environment. People are keen to impress and worry that they're not pulling their weight, but my thinking when I started this job was this: "Be good enough" – I wasn't a perfect parent so why would I aspire to be the perfect employee? "Good enough" on both fronts, was how I was going to make it work.

Anya was about to go to nursery, so Harry and I worked out that I'd do pick up and he'd take her in the mornings. So for the first three months, whilst I established myself, I would work the 12-hour days, getting to the office at 5 am working till 5 pm and then picking up Anya. The pay rise was substantial enough that it was worth it for this short period of time. I made a conscious decision that I'd go without sleep. So I'd have 5 hours a night – 11 pm till 4 am – and I coped for that short time.

As time went on I found I didn't need to do the 12-hour day every day. I had autonomy for the first time and nobody needed to know where I was all the time as long as the work got done. As I got better at my job and faster at it, I would sometimes get there at 6 am but leave at 3 pm – life got easier.

The problem was, the nursery was a bit rigid, so on the days I did work later, I struggled to get back to the nursery in time for the pick up. So, we had to switch to a nanny.

In the end I got one final raise and it meant that Harry's salary was covering the nanny, so he could give up work if he wanted to. He jumped at the chance, he wanted to do it immediately! He has never been as bothered by work as I am.

Harry's so much better as a stay-at-home parent than I'd ever be. He's class rep, he gets on with all the mums and organizes a Friday play date. Neither of us feels like we're jacking in something we love ...

Now because I manage projects I don't have to be there all the time, there's nobody watching you – and every now and then I take the afternoon off – I went to the cinema the other afternoon and nobody batted an eyelid. You don't sit with a team and you don't have a line manager.

My original kamikaze of 5 am to 5 pm didn't last long. There's a role for me when I get home: I do bath, homework, bedtime which I love because I've really missed Anya all day. It works perfectly now – we're perfectly happy. I never thought when I took the money it'd mean one of us could give up our job.'

SO WHAT CAN I DO ABOUT THIS INEQUALITY, IMBALANCE OF WORKLOAD?

You're probably thinking: not much. I can't change the ludicrous cost of childcare, I can't undo centuries of gender stereotypes. I might as well do everything (and continue to feel totally overwhelmed) because that's just the way it is. But there are things you can do: the first and most important being to actually think about how you could do it differently.

> 66 **One of the main reasons people stay in their crazy, busy lives, is because they can't seem to find the time to think about how to change them. So we keep spinning faster and faster, and assume change is impossible. I know I did.** 99
>
> Brigid Schulte, author of *Overwhelmed*

BRIGID SCHULTE ON FINDING EQUALITY AT HOME

'Tom and I had done pretty well dividing chores fairly when it was just the two of us. But once we had the kids, the scales started tipping and though we'd try and right them every now and then, usually after I'd lost it, I always ended up feeling I was in charge of everything.

The crisis point came at Thanksgiving one year, where rather than helping me with the preparation of a meal for 18 guests, Tom strolled into the kitchen and announced he was going over to a friends to help him with the turkey (i.e. put it in the smoker and sit on the patio drinking beer). I was livid.

Desperate to find another way, I met Jessica De Groot who runs "Third Path Institute" in Philadelphia, which helps couples try to find a more integrated approach to work and life.

Travelling the third path helped me to see that to right family systems like mine, so precariously off balance, requires challenging enormously powerful cultural expectations of who we are and how we're supposed to act: the "work-devoted ideal worker", the self-sacrificing ideal mother, and the distant provider father. These are the long-held norms we hold in our heads about how things should be, and they are what get us into the overwhelm – and the overwhelm prevents us from finding a way out.

"When couples are angry with each other, standing in their living rooms fighting about ways to create more time, they don't realize that there are these other invisible forces in the room with them", says De Groot. "The Ideal mother, the provider father and the ideal worker are right there, pulling the strings."

So what happens? Couples get stuck because they feel they don't have a choice or another path. "Choice requires having meaningful alternatives," says De Groot "and so many couples don't think there are any."'

"Making our to-do lists equal really helped" – *Rachael*

'My husband Jon and I had always prided ourselves on sharing things equally when it was just the two of us. But then we had our three daughters and the balance somehow tipped. I had five years off work between the second and the third child – then I went back to work part time which is when the issue became most evident. I started to realize I'd be either working all day or doing childcare, as well as all the domestic and kids stuff in the evening, and it started to feel unfair.

Jon works hard as a marketing director, but in terms of the sheer amount of stuff that needed to be done every day and the time available to do it in, I was getting by far the biggest load. I didn't really see why I should be doing an online supermarket shop and all the cooking in the evening whilst he messed around on the Internet! We both had jobs and so I felt we should share the other stuff. I felt like I had to contain a million things in my head at one time – whilst all he had to do was go to work.

It got to a point where it felt like so many things had to be done in a 24-hour period and none of them were happening. I was getting so frustrated as I constantly felt like I wasn't keeping up.

Eventually we sat down and talked about it. Jon just hadn't realized how much I was doing – he agreed it was unfair and we worked out a plan. We wrote down a list of all the things we have to get done in a day and then made his list and my list more equal.

This made the load I had to think about lighter, and the atmosphere in the house a lot more pleasant! Equally, talking about it made me realize that if it was going to work and things be shared more equally, I had to resist the temptation to "micro-manage" Jon and let him actually get on and do it his way. We realized it was also important, however, to play to one another's strengths and make decisions as a couple a lot more.'

In summary, then, we can see how dissatisfaction, confusion over roles or resentment that we are somehow not able to fulfil our potential, all lead to a fairly catastrophic lack of focus. It basically comes down to unhappiness: if we are unhappy with our lot – our home/work balance or set-up – and can't seem to find a way around it, we lose our way and this can have a very negative impact on our lives and our relationships. In fact, it often causes them to break down.

This is why it's so important to communicate and to TALK. Whether that be with your partner, spouse, boss or parents – it's only by talking things through with people that we can:

- see and consider options we may not have seen before;
- hear the other side of the story (their opinion), which can give us very useful insights and help us to solve the issues;
- find the 'third way' that is right for us.

Each person's circumstances are so different that there really is no set of templates. The only way you are going to get your life focus back on track and most importantly feel happier, is if you talk. Sounds so simple, doesn't it? But as we know, the simplest things are pretty much always the most effective and 'a problem shared is a problem halved' has to be one of the truest statements going when it comes to trying to carve out a life that works better for us.

SIX STEPS TO THE 'THIRD WAY'

As we've said, there is no template, but follow these guidelines to kick-starting your discussion about how to get your roles and your life working the way you want them:

- Break free of social norms that straitjacket men and women into different roles – the 'ideal worker' the 'ideal mother' – and find a way that works for YOU.
- Remember: men want to share parenting.
- Actually talk (it's amazing how few people do) about what you both expect from work, kids and home and also about what you both want.
- Agree to common standards and seek to divide work fairly.

This could also mean removing 'mental clutter' (contaminated time). When Jessica De Groot's husband said, 'What do you want for dinner?' She said 'Not to have to think about it.' It's that 'having to think about everything' that fugs up our minds and erodes our focus.

Each person needs to take their specific tasks (be that loading the dishwasher or being the main childcarer) and be responsible for them – own them.

See http://www.thirdpath.org for loads more ideas and resources.

ASK YOURSELF

 How happy are you with the gender balance in your household? Have you ever sat down and discussed how you'd both like it to be? Or whether it's working as it is?

 It's more efficient if people play to their strengths, so decide who is good at what in terms of domestic duties and chores.

 What – if any – 'ideal roles' do you carry around in your head that could be holding you back? (i.e. 'ideal wife' 'ideal father'). Is there a third/alternative way for you too?

How could you make time – even just 5 minutes a day – to think about the balance in your life and whether/how you want to change things?

CHAPTER 6

FOCUS ROBBERS

e understand that one of the symptoms of feeling overwhelmed and unfocused is not being able to see the wood for the trees. You want to change, but you want to be told how in a way that doesn't fry your head further. You need less information, not more. You need the right information.

We have tried to keep this book simple and show you how anybody can learn how to be more focused. To do this you need to recognize how and why you've lost your focus and then put in place strategies to hunt yours down. If you take away only one thing from this book, let it be our comprehensive list of Focus Robbers.

Just think, simply by banishing a few of these from your life today, you'll improve your focus no end.

1. VICTIM MENTALITY

We know, sometimes, that the only thing for it is a good moan: 'Poor me, I'm so busy and overwhelmed/my life is so stressful.' Of course it often feels this way, but this negative thinking pattern only exacerbates feelings of being overwhelmed. Perceiving our own lives as a threat means our bodies release cortisol, and this causes us to spiral, spectacularly, into unproductive 'headless chicken' mode.

Even when things are going well, we fixate on how we now have lots more to work on, rather than on the fact that things are actually going well for us. But if you feel frazzled, do something productive about it. Make a time log to see where your time is going and how you might carve out some more, because at the end of the day, whatever life you choose, we're all stressed some of the time. The important thing is to notice the upsides of the choices you make and recognize the positive things in your life too.

Make a daily gratitude list: three good things that happened today. After a while you'll find you start to look for them.

2. OVERCOMMITTING

It's very tempting to say 'yes' to everything. You worry that if you don't:

- You won't be asked again (FOMO – Fear of Missing Out).
- People will think you're lazy.
- People won't like you.

But taking on more than you realistically have time to do has a domino effect: your stress levels soar, meaning you lose focus (straight into fight or flight mode); you fail to complete the task or do it well and risk letting other people down. As time management expert Mark Forster puts it: 'The question these days shouldn't be what am I going to take on, it's what I am *not* going to take on? So ask yourself if you take this on, are you going to be able to do it well? Otherwise it kind of defeats the object.'

Forster uses a car analogy: 'Every part of a car is important, you can't say you'll do the seats but not the engine; the gears but not the breaks. If you don't have time, don't take on any more cars, so you can produce the ones you've committed to, well.'

The thing is, once we've said 'yes' it's very difficult to backtrack; and we find ourselves, at 4 am, in that awful *why on earth did I say yes to this?* head spin. The answer? 'Say no at the commitment level, not the task level.'

Say 'no' at the outset.

3. TELLING YOURSELF UNTRUTHS

It's very easy when we're stressed, hurt or overwhelmed to make up stories in our heads. This is just our way of trying to make sense of things; literally giving our problems a beginning, middle and end. The problem is, these stories we tell ourselves are often not true and can even be damaging – especially to our focus. When Vanderkam wrote her book *I Know How She Does It* she interviewed hundreds of women and asked them to keep a time log. She also heard the stories they told themselves about their lives. What she found was that these were often untrue: 'I met women who worked full-time in demanding jobs and felt permanently guilty about how much time they spent seeing their kids,' she explains. 'They'd say to me, "I never see my kids", but when they sat down and wrote their time logs, they saw they spent 35 hours a week with their kids. If you spend 35 hours in the office, you wouldn't say "I never see the office".' These stories we tell ourselves can damage our self-esteem and set us back. Also, beware of looking for evidence to support your claims. Psychologists call it 'confirmation bias': I feel like I never see my kids, becomes hunting for evidence that your kids are suffering, for example.

Challenge the stories you tell yourself.

> 66 **If you're going to search for evidence to back up your theories, make sure the theories are positive.** 99

Laura Vanderkam, author and speaker

4. PERFECTIONISM

> 66 **Having ridiculously high domestic standards will eat into your leisure time. Nobody cares if your house is spotless.** 99

Laura Vanderkam, author and speaker

We all like to have high standards, but if you let your 'everything needs to be perfect' tendencies take hold they can rob you of your focus and stop you doing what's truly important. You start to procrastinate: 'I can't start work until my desk is perfectly arranged', 'I can't play Lego with you because I'm making you pesto from scratch'. If this sounds familiar, then it could be that your high standards are to blame for your feelings of being overwhelmed. You feel like you can't keep up with the demands of your life. But who is setting the demands? You might feel you have to live in a spotless house, for example, and feel like you never sit down; but is it someone else demanding this from you – or just you?

Take a look at your standards – are they unnecessarily high?

5. TRYING TO DO EVERYTHING YOURSELF

> **❝Could you imagine Steve Jobs worrying about the logistics, or about the parking or the stationery? No. He played to his strengths and let everybody else do the stuff they are good at.❞**
>
> Sháá Wasmund, MBE, speaker, entrepreneur and author

It may be tempting to come over all proud and think 'it'll only get done if I do it myself' but this is just another form of overcommitting and a recipe for loss of focus. Not to mention bad management. Know yourself and your strengths and devote your time to the stuff *only* you can do. If you spread yourself too thin, you may run the risk of failing to do the ONE thing you are employed to do.

Do the things only you are truly good at and leave the rest to the people who do it better.

6. NOT TAKING BREAKS

"Don't assume that working longer is working better – because it very often isn't."

Brigid Schulte, author of *Overwhelmed*

You've got loads on and a deadline to meet, so what do you do? Just keep on working, right? You don't have time to be taking breaks. Actually, there is a growing body of scientific evidence that says we are much more productive and focused when we do. It's very simple: when we work the brain, it burns through glucose and, if we don't give it chance to recover, we get depleted fast. After all, the brain is like any other part of our body. If we continue to use it, it becomes fatigued and needs a rest period before it can recover and be at its optimum.

Try working in 90-minute pulses or doing the Pomodoro Effect (see Chapter 2).

7. NOT SCHEDULING THINGS THAT NEED TO HAPPEN

We all do it: 'Oh we must meet up for lunch!' Two years later, we still haven't met up for lunch. Intentions are all well and good but that's all they are – intentions. If you don't make a firm commitment to do something, chances are it just won't happen. And this doesn't have to mean just work-related stuff. Not scheduling things we want to do in our leisure time ensures they don't happen either. And then we just fritter away time doing lots of energy-sapping activities like watching TV and browsing the Net.

If you keep making promises to lunch with someone who matters to you and it never happens, call them today and don't come off the phone until you've scheduled them in! Worried your friends might think you're treating them like a business client by 'scheduling' them in? Think again. 'Tell them, I'm not treating you as a business client,' says Sháá Wasmund, 'I'm treating you like you're important.'

Call a friend you've been meaning to see for ages today, and schedule a meet-up.

8. CONFUSING BUSYNESS WITH PRODUCTIVITY

It's very easy to be busy, to be constantly doing things, but much harder to be productive; and we often fill our time with trivial things when we're overwhelmed because the effort it takes to really achieve things seems all too much effort. If you've ever decided to clear out the kitchen drawer to avoid doing that presentation you have a deadline for, you'll understand what we mean. Don't fall into the 'busy trap' of doing more and achieving less. Whenever you do something, you should always have something to show for it at the end.

Pick ONE important thing you want to get done today and don't do any of the other stuff until it's done.

9. PEOPLE PLEASING

Often, the reason we don't manage to spend time with the people who really matter is because we're far too busy trying to please those who don't; going for coffee with someone because we feel we 'should', promising to help that person with their job search when they're not giving anything in return. Sháá Wasmund suggests following the 20/80 rule: decide who makes up the top 20 per cent of people who matter in your life and schedule them in. This doesn't mean you should never see the other 80 per cent: you simply have to prioritize the 20 per cent first.

Dr Tamara Russell also suggests dropping the 'should' monkey. 'If you find yourself saying "I really should do this, or should see that person" – take a rain check. Do you really have to?'

Prioritize the people who matter/learn to say no to those who don't.

10. NOT BEING REALISTIC

This one is about expectations: if we are not realistic about what and how much we can do and expect too much of ourselves, then we set ourselves up for failure. Doubt creeps in and we lose our focus. The answer? Constantly 'prune' your life, says Sháá Wasmund:

> *'If you want something to grow you have to prune back the bad weeds so that the nutrients can get to the bits that will give you the best rewards – it's the same with life. If you have a gym membership but never go, stop it … start running alongside your child instead when they are cycling to school.'*

Also, get analytical and review what's going wrong. If you feel you're constantly falling short on your daily tasks or your goals, ask yourself whether you are simply trying to do too much, or if you are setting unrealistic deadlines. Ask yourself: is this a deadline I can push back on? Often it can be, but the difficulty lies in having the courage to say no or to push back. However, if you keep saying 'yes, I'll do that' without thinking realistically about whether it is achievable, people will continue to pile things onto you.

Be compassionate with yourself first and you'll be able to be more generous with other people.

Look at what gives you the best rewards in life and cut back on the rest. Try to make your expectations realistic.

The list of Focus Robbers in this chapter is obviously not comprehensive. There are many more habits, distractions and attitudes that rob us of the ability to focus; we've merely tried to present you with the some of the most common. Similarly, not all of these examples above will relate to you. If we were to try and address all of them it would defeat the object of this whole book since you would very likely become overwhelmed! The trick – and the way you'll get the most out of this chapter – is to be aware, when you're reading each of them, which ones you're nodding at the most and thinking to yourself, aha, that sounds familiar! Start with those or that one – start working on it today. Real Focus, after all, is very much about taking baby steps towards one big goal.

ASK YOURSELF

 Am I achieving the goals I set for myself? If not, why not?

 Could I lower my standards or expectations to be more realistic?

 Of all the Focus Robbers, how many do I recognize as being guilty of myself?

 Which two Focus Robbers could I choose to work on improving in the coming week?

3 HOW CAN YOU BECOME MORE FOCUSED?

CHAPTER 7

DO WHAT MATTERS

s we've already discussed, 'doing what matters' really is the crux of Real Focus. If you take anything at all away from this book, make it this. It makes sense that a focused life, a life lived well, is as full as possible of the things that are important to us (and contains as little as possible of the things that aren't: ironing anyone? tax returns?).

This is what we call 'the good life' and it's something we're certain anyone can have when they know how. At the beginning of *I Know How She Does It*, Laura Vanderkam regales her readers with a poignant tale. Whilst visiting a strawberry-picking farm, she was taken by the words on the baskets that visitors were given to put their strawberries in: *Remember the berry season is short. This box holds approximately 10 lbs level full.* This struck Vanderkam as a metaphor for life: in other words, since the basket only holds so much, what will you choose to fill it with? What is important to you?

And more importantly, you may be asking yourself: how do I find out?

KNOW YOURSELF

Deeper self-awareness and self-knowledge is our key to getting to the heart of what makes us tick and what really matters to us. Socrates said 'know thyself' but it's surprising how few of us really do. 'Be authentic' is the message we hear so often – but some find that easier than others, especially in a work situation where we may have cultivated a persona without even really realizing it, perhaps in order to maintain an identity that is different from home. Also, we are not just our own thoughts. We are an amalgamation of our past experiences, our parents' values and expectations, society's expectations and many other factors. It's for this reason that being 'true to ourselves' and, essentially, doing what matters is not black and white.

What it comes down to, however – the *point* of knowing yourself, if you like – is gaining more meaning in your life. Meaning is really what we all seek. After all, what is the point without it? What does it all mean?! Once we are able to lead lives with real meaning, we will automatically be more focused. The two exist hand in hand, parallel to one another: by being focused, we find meaning, and once we have meaning we're able to be more focused.

So how does one find meaning? Asking yourself these four basic questions may well be a good place to start and may be more difficult than you thought. Spend some time on them. The results could be hugely enlightening.

1. What's important to you? (core values)

Our core values are at the centre of who we really are – they define us. They are deeply held beliefs that guide our behaviour, help us make decisions and do what's important. In a way, we could say that our core values ARE what's important to us deep down. They are motivate us to get up in the morning and give our life meaning and purpose. We know this, because when we're not being faithful to them, we don't feel as if we're growing as a person or reaching our potential. When you feel you've 'lost your way' it's usually because you're not being true to your core values. The good news is that being in alignment with our values – living the life we want – is not just the secret to focus, but also fulfillment, contentment and even joy.

The first step, however, is finding out what your core values really are. Everyone has core values, but you may just not have identified yours yet, or know how to. (Help is at hand!)

SHÁÁ WASMUND'S GUIDE TO FINDING YOUR CORE VALUES

'Before you can "walk your talk", you need to figure out what's really important to you. Only then will you know who you truly are and be capable of living an authentic life.

I'm not talking riches here, not financial riches anyway, because all the money in the world won't make you happy if you're not living your life your way. I'm talking about the unwritten rules and regulations that you live your life by, without even thinking about it. So how do you determine what they are? Start with asking yourself a few questions, then make notes of your answers and list them in order of priority. The ones at the top are your core values.

1. *What is my greatest asset? Why?*
2. *What really matters to you? What are the most important things to you in life?*
3. *What do you love doing? What do you enjoy doing the most?*
4. *Can you remember the last time you felt super energized? What were you doing?*
5. *What annoys, frustrates or upsets you?*

By exploring your answers to these questions, you'll start to get a sense of what's really important to you. On answering the first four, delve deeper and ask yourself what each of these give you – this in turn should help to define a core value. For example: I've always said my support network is my greatest asset. I would be nothing without the loyal people in my life. I call them my 3 am friends. Take a step back and ask yourself if you're truly prepared to show up for people the way you would want them to show up for you ... So for me, LOYALTY is one of my core values.

With your answer to the fifth and final question, you can turn this on its head to reveal your value. For example, if you feel upset from seeing a homeless person on the street, someone being bullied at work, or an elderly person standing on the train, this probably points to your core values being around empathy and ethics.'

2. What are you good at? (strengths)

We all have strengths, and Real Focus is about tapping into those and maximizing them. It's when we're playing to our strengths that we can really get 'in flow'. Strengths can be actual talents – designing, maths, writing – but equally, they can be personal qualities that are sometimes harder to identify or be aware of yourself. Perhaps you have charisma and are the sort of person who can talk to anyone, or you're a good listener or very persuasive. If you're not sure where your strengths lie, ask yourself what other people compliment you on, or ask you to do. Even ask a couple of people close to you what they think your strengths are (a family member and a colleague perhaps), because very often other people can see things we can't.

Another thing to bear in mind is that our strengths are often things that come easier to us. So a question also worth asking is what do I really enjoy doing? (Because these things tend to come easier too!)

> **❝ People who use their strengths every day are six times more likely to be engaged in their work. ❞**
>
> Sháá Wasmund, MBE, speaker, entrepreneur and author

3. What excites and inspires you? (passions)

It makes sense that when we're doing what we love, things feel a whole lot easier. But also we are far less likely to become distracted or go looking for distractions if we're engaged in something we're really enjoying. It may be that you've lost sight of what excites and inspires you and need to find that again in order to find your focus. So spend some time thinking about what you love doing – both in terms of work but also pleasure – because often you can marry the two. For example, you might love meeting new people and being outdoors, or looking after people and doing craft. These things can probably be amalgamated with a bit of creative thinking. But don't think finding your passion has to mean with regards to what job you do. Introducing more things you're passionate about in your free time is just as rewarding and uplifting and could even lead you to your dream job in the end.

4. What do you want? (vision)

So you've defined your core values – what matters most to you. Vision is really about what your aspirations are for the future and your core values and passions should support this vision. What do you want to accomplish? What is all this work, paid or otherwise (perhaps you have vision to run a marathon for example, or write a novel) ultimately contributing towards? If you imagine yourself in one, five, ten years' time, what do you hope to be doing? Imagine you are meeting your best friend from school in a year's time. Write your dream conversation: what would you ideally want to be telling him or her about where you are in life and what you've achieved?

When starting to work out what is important to you, it's probable that the following will come up in some way:

* Meaningful work.
* Love – family/romantic.
* Leisure.

However, clearly it's not 'one size fits all' – we are all individuals. So what can you do to get to the core of what really matters for you?

MARK FORSTER ON HOW TO WORK OUT WHAT YOU *REALLY* WANT

'So much about focus is asking yourself the right questions:

1. Choose a day to take five minutes and ask yourself: what do I really want?

2. Write a list of, say, ten items on your computer or in a notebook. They can be general – for example things you want to achieve in your career/a holiday you want to take/a hobby you'd like to try. Or, you can make it as focused as you wish, asking yourself: what do I really want in my romantic life? What shall I do with my family this summer holidays? It works for everything.

3. Repeat the exercise the next day but don't refer to the day before's list – make a fresh one. Repeat for a week.

So how and why does this work?

1. By repeating the exercise every day for a week instead of just doing it once, you allow "refining" to happen. You refine your list so that it reflects the truth more as the days go on. You get to the very 'core' of what you want.

2. This is because once your brain is given a problem it begins to work on it to come up with the best solution. If you were to do just one list, on one day, you wouldn't be giving your brain that "percolating" time to work out the best solutions, so the list would be very superficial.

3. Much of the work is done between each list-making event. It's a bit like weight-lifting – most of the changes and improvement to the muscles happens between training sessions, and it's the same with making this list; the unconscious works on it overnight.

4. *Most of our to-do lists are full of things we think are important "right now". They tend to be fossilized. Longer and longer, and full of stuff that we never get round to; by the time we get round to completing many of the tasks (if we ever do) they aren't important anymore. This is why to-do lists quickly become stale, and we end up with 50 items with only the last 2 relevant to our lives. This is the reason why, with this exercise, you shouldn't look at the day before's list when you make the new day's: anything that's truly important you will remember – if you have to refer to a list, it's probably not really what matters to you!*

5. *You will probably find as the list-making goes on you become braver, more creative and more authentic in what you write down. This is because we tend to write only things we're expected to at the beginning. We also feel motivated by what we write down, and start to make some of them happen ...'*

In summary then, it's out with the 'to-do' list and in with the 'What do I WANT to do list?', i.e. what is important to me? Perhaps the reason that so many things on our to-do lists don't ever get done and our lists become – as Forster puts it – 'fossilized' is because there are things on there we think we should do rather than things that truly matter to us. When we focus on these things, life feels much more 'in flow' and all-round easier!

The new to-do list

You can take the above concept of list making and apply it to your daily to-do list too. In fact throwaway your to-do list (shock horror!) and start doing this instead:

- Make a daily list of five things only at the beginning of each day that you need to achieve.

- Start at the beginning and move down the list (always in the order they appear, don't prioritize). Everything that's on the list should be there because it's important – otherwise, why is it on the list?
- As you achieve each thing, cross it off.
- If you don't achieve it, cross it off and put it at the top of the list.
- Start again with the same list the next day – not adding anything else until you have done the thing at the top of the list.

Doing this means that 'fossilizing' of your to-do list can't and won't happen because no item is allowed to linger on the bottom of the list like the one soggy vegetable that always seems to linger at the bottom of your fridge. Anything that doesn't get done that day goes straight to the top of the list for the next day, meaning it definitely gets done. The fact that you don't add any more items until the thing at the top is done – and then you only add ONE item – means you keep your list permanently at five items only.

CHANNEL YOUR INNER CHILD

Left to their own devices, children tend to only do the things they love. This is because a sense of duty or 'I should do this because it's good for me' hasn't set in yet. It's all about the pleasure! Unfortunately, as we get older, responsibilities mean we do more of what we have to do and sometimes the things we love get pushed out or forgotten about. But chances are, what you loved doing when you were nine is what you love doing now given the chance – it's just a case of remembering it. Think about it: did you love to dance? Sing? Build things? What's stopping you doing those things now?

PUTTING IT INTO PRACTICE

So, hopefully after reading this chapter you've got a much better idea of what matters to you. How do you put it into practice? How do you make that leap from knowing something in theory to making things a reality?

Find your 'sweet spot'

Think of your 'sweet spot' as the optimum place for you to be (it's usually work-related, i.e. your ideal job, but it can mean in life in general too). It is basically the intersection where the following meet:

- Your skills: what are you good at? What comes easily to you?

- Your interests: what do you like talking about the most/doing/ dreaming or reading about?

- Your opportunities: this is the slightly trickier one, as we can't manufacture or magic up opportunities. However, we *can* cultivate a life where more opportunities are likely to arise. This means broadening your social circle, going to networking events, keeping up with the blogs/websites/social media in your field. Be proactive rather than reactive: don't wait for opportunities to arise, create them for yourself: write to companies telling them what you can do for them, rather than asking if they have any work.

Work with intention

Academics say there are two types of work: 'Work with Obligation' and 'Work with Intention'. We probably don't need to explain the former (the word 'obligation' speaks for itself!). But what is 'Work with Intention'? You know, those projects where it's not about the money and you're willing to pull an all-nighter to finish it, simply because you love it? That's 'Work with Intention' and it also probably means you've found your sweet-spot.

The magic really happens in these roles because it's where we're doing what really matters to us; it's where our passions, core values and vision collide. If we can find a way to focus on doing 'work with intention' more often than not, it follows that we are far more likely to make an impact in the areas of work that matter to us most.

! SURROUND YOURSELF WITH PEOPLE WHO INSPIRE YOU

Remember that buzzy feeling you get after being around certain people? You laugh more, you enjoy it more, you feel like your life is just that tiny bit richer for seeing them? Surround yourself as much as possible in the company of these people – they'll make it easier for you to stay focused.

Find your 'flow'

What is it?

We've all heard of the familiar phrase – 'time flies when you're having fun' – and this could be said to describe perfectly the state of being 'in flow', that being 'in the zone' feeling where you're so immersed in what you are doing, you don't notice the time passing; or in fact anything else other than what you're doing.

First coined by psychologist Mihaly Csikszentmihalyi, 'being in flow' is considered by many other academics to be the secret to true happiness. This is because, by its very nature, when we're in a state of flow, we are actually unable to worry or ruminate about anything. The brain can't do both at the same time, and being 'in flow' is so absorbing that it can't help but choose that option.

People are thought to experience genuine contentment and satisfaction when in flow. Psychologists have called it the 'optimal life experience' or 'most desirable state in the world'.

How do you know you're in it?

- You know you're in flow or in the zone, because the work almost seems to be doing itself.
- You feel challenged but never overwhelmed.
- You feel immersed but aren't clock watching or even aware of the time.
- More than anything, you feel stimulated and engaged.
- You have increased energy.
- You feel as if you are playing to your strengths.

Being in flow = being as focused as we are able to be. Everything 'just works', meaning optimum productivity.

How can I get in flow?

Being in flow does not mean there is no effort involved – quite the contrary. In fact, the state of 'flow' sits only on the very fine line between the difficulty of the task and the skill of the performer. If something is too easy for our skill level, we're likely to become bored; likewise, if it's too hard, we're likely to be discouraged. The key to flow is doing something that's just about possible for us to achieve if we really put our minds to it – it's about really challenging ourselves, but not trying to achieve the impossible. It's about 'self-mastery' – that is being in control of ourselves; our thoughts, our actions and our habits.

Some scientists say that 'in flow' is where we tap into our inner genius because it's where our inner critic is silenced, meaning we are more focused and productive than ever.

In fact, people who experience flow often are said to experience more self-esteem and greater life fulfillment. Sounds pretty good, doesn't it? So how can you help yourself get there? Or at least increase your chances of entering 'FLOW'?

1. Skills need to be well-matched to the task – all this means is that you're up to the job. It might be challenging but you have the skills to do it. It follows that if you've never been taught to use Excel that you're not going to get in 'flow' setting up a complicated spreadsheet, for example!

2. Being in the moment – we are going to explore this further in Chapter 9, but basically this means that you need to be 100 per cent focused on the task in hand to get into flow, which may mean switching off email/your phone. It means using what is already there, rather than thinking of things you need to do or should have done.

3. You need to have clear goals. This is the 'vision' thing again. Setting out with a clear idea of what you'd like to accomplish when you've finished the task or job will keep you going in the direction you need to be travelling and means you are therefore far more likely to achieve 'flow'.

4. You need to be able to focus on the journey as well as the goal – this is really about self-mastery again and self-awareness. Listen to your thoughts as they arise; think about your thinking as you're doing the task, be the master of your mind. It's yours, after all.

REAL PEOPLE

"How I learnt to do what matters" – *Ben*

'After I graduated from law school, I got a job as a litigation lawyer at KPMG – a big accountancy firm in the City. In my 20s, it was really exciting. The money was great, I was doing well and they kept promoting me.

Sadly, when I was 30, one of the guys I worked with – a good friend – got ill with leukaemia and died leaving two children. He was a partner of the firm – it was where I would have been in 4–5 years' time. It made me realize that time was precious, and made me wonder, do I want to still be doing this job? Time could be short, you just never know what's around the corner.

Initially, I thought the answer was to work for a smaller company with a less capitalist ethos; and so I got a new job doing this, and handed in my notice at KPMG. When my boss subsequently asked what would make me stay, I said "a four-day week".

They were very taken aback! It was unheard of for men – let alone, a man without a child – to ask for a four-day working week. But they agreed to this, as well as offering a pay rise, and more travel, so I couldn't refuse!

There was definitely stigma about not being a "serious player" anymore – but I didn't care. Ultimately, having a better life balance was beginning to be more important to me. I used to love having a pint with lunch about midday on a Friday whilst everyone rushed past in a suit. I got a three-day weekend, which was wonderful, as I'd cook and do things I enjoyed. I also began buying and doing up property, which created an alternative income.

Eventually, I had four buy-to-let properties which meant I had enough money to give up work. So I went to Spain for three months, then returned do a TEFL (Teaching English as a Foreign Language) course and became a language teacher for a short time.

It was then that I met my son's mother (our son came along two years later). Becoming a father, I realized, was finally the meaning in life I'd been searching for – this was what was important.

The alternative income I had from properties meant that I was able to give up work so that I could do what I really wanted – to spend time with my son.

Seven years on, I've never looked back or been happier. I'm much happier pottering in the garden and doing the childcare than sitting at a desk all day – even if I have much less money. I've found a way to make it work for me.'

ASK YOURSELF

 What did I love doing when I was a child? What were my passions?

 Looking at my time log/time diary: what's missing? What do I want to see more of?

 If I had six months to live, what would I focus on? More importantly, what would I leave out?

 What am I good at? What do I love? What do people ask me to help them with?

 When was the last time I felt in 'flow'? What was I doing at the time?

CHAPTER 8

RECLAIM YOUR TIME

e talked in Chapter 1 about 'time confetti' – that state we find ourselves in where our time feels fragmented and bitty, projects get started but not finished, and we never seem to have big enough chunks of time to devote to what's important.

We all know people for whom life doesn't seem to be like this. For whom time seems to work differently. In our minds, these people live rich and balanced lives; they do an outstanding job at work and seem to fit in all the other things they love to do also, and at the same time still manage to have a life.

You may well wonder how on earth they achieve so much more than you – considering you both have the same number of hours in the day. What's their secret?

The truth is, there isn't one. They've probably simply mastered a few simple basics of Real Focus – like prioritizing what matters and good time management. They get so much done because they're discerning about *what* they do. Rather than spreading themselves too thinly and trying to do everything, they just do the things that matter to them and, also, the right thing at the right time. The good news is that all this is within your reach too – it's just having the tools at your disposal.

In this chapter, we're going to look more closely at how to not just manage your time, but invest in it and use it wisely, focusing on the things that are truly important to you. It's about doing less but more of the right stuff, basically, so that you too can be one of those people you may have previously envied!

KNOW WHERE YOUR TIME GOES

The first step in acquiring any new skill, or improving on one, is awareness. It's only once we're aware of things that we can make changes in our lives, strengthen our weak areas and play to our strengths. The same goes for time management, or as Sháá

Wasmund likes to call it, 'investing in our time'. How can you use your time more wisely if you don't know where it all goes in the first place? If you're not aware of how you spend it? The first step in budgeting would be knowing what you spend your money on – we can apply the same notion to being more careful and efficient with our time.

Keeping track of your time and where it goes is as much a skill as managing it well, and if anyone can tell you how best to do this, it has to be author and speaker Laura Vanderkam. As a researcher in how people spend their time, Vanderkam noticed that many women seemed to tell themselves they couldn't 'have it all' if 'all' meant children and a big job. Vanderkam wanted to challenge this notion, and so she set out on a quest to find out how, women who *did* do both (earned more than $100,000 a year and had at least one child living at home) made it work.

She made a time log sheet on Excel – basically the 24-hour day split into half-hour cells – and asked the women to fill it in, going into as much detail as possible about what they were doing in that time slot. She called this project the 'Mosaic Project' since the half-hour slots were like tiles on a mosaic. Filled in, Vanderkam was able to see, in black and white, where the women's time went and how all the tiles fitted together to make a life that worked. The time diary study was 1,001 days in the lives of professional women and their families.

So what did she find? In general, she found that, contrary to the belief their lives might be a nightmare as they juggled a million things at once, actually their lives were pretty good – and crucially, that this notion that the big jobs were off limits for them, was unfounded.

> 'It's all in how you perceive "having it all". If that is having a job you enjoy and a family and friends and leisure time, then you can have it all. If it's having a full-on job and no childcare, then you probably can't. You have to be realistic – otherwise you feel overwhelmed.'

As Vanderkam explains, she was interested in the whole picture, the whole 'mosaic' of people's lives. Rather than seeing our lives as 9–5 followed by the evening, Vanderkam encourages us to see it as 48 (half-hours) tiles with which to play with; to move around as we wish. When we start to think of our time like this, it can feel quite liberating. We begin to see our days as lots of different pockets of time that we can use and move around at will, rather than two immovable blocks of time (the day and the evening).

This opens up so many more possibilities in terms of how we use our time, and allows us to be a lot more flexible and experimental – 'curators' of our own ideal lives. But it's not that we have any more time, it's simply that we are being more creative in using what we have. Boiled down, the 'mosaic' approach is really just a matter of changing our perceptions, but it's (perhaps strangely, a bit like magic!) a very effective one.

LAURA VANDERKAM ON HOW TO KEEP AND USE A TIME LOG

1. *'Using an Excel spreadsheet, put the days of the week at the top and the time in half-hour cells down the left-hand side, starting from when you get up to when you go to bed.*

2. *Fill it in, in as much detail as possible for a week, being as specific as you can. It's important to be this detailed, so you can really see where all those hours go!*

3. *When analysing it after a week, look at what you'd like to see more of and also less of.*

4. *What needs improvement? What's disappointing? Do you, for example, feel like you could use your evenings better?'*

PROTECT YOUR TIME

Some might say that time is the most valuable commodity we have, but so is our energy. Even if we had all the time in the world to do what we wanted, if we don't reserve our energies to use it wisely and to greatest effect, we risk wasting that time and losing focus on the tasks or activities that are really important to us. In this way, our time may be our most valuable commodity, but our energy is possibly the greatest currency we have. We only have so much, after all, and it needs to be treated with respect.

One of the key reasons for time and energy wasting is not having firm enough boundaries around them. Boundaries are basically what's ok and what's not ok – i.e. what you are comfortable spending your time and energy doing, and what you are not.

Sometimes, however, we only realize what our limits are when they're tested. It's then that we need to really listen to our feelings and there that our boundaries need to be placed.

Imagine, for example, that you get asked to travel two hours to meet a potential client, or you make a new friend who then expects you to have coffee with him or her once a week. You will know what your own limits are – and therefore where your boundaries should be – by how you feel: feeling discomfort or resentment are two big indicators that your boundaries have been crossed, and we all have every right to reinforce them.

Having healthy boundaries to protect our store of energy, then, is so important. How can we retain enough energy to focus and do the things that matter, if we spend all our energies on things we don't want to do, but feel obliged to? Or on looking after everyone but ourselves?

Also, having healthy boundaries improves our self-esteem, and we work a whole lot better when we feel good about ourselves. Giving out the message that your own feelings and needs matter encourages other people to think the same. Also, being a martyr is good for nobody – neither you NOR the other person. Setting boundaries is done out of respect and compassion for the other person too. People have every right to ask for what they want but you have every right to decide if it's right and convenient for YOU.

Ways to cultivate healthier boundaries now

1. **Notice people that drain you and limit your time with them.**

   We all have different kinds of 'energy' and some people's energies simply don't complement our own. Think if it as having your own personal engine. Some are big and powerful and built for speed; some are more suited to going at a leisurely pace.

   There's also the question of 'wavelength' when we feel drained or irritable after spending time with someone – it's often nobody's fault, it's just that we're on different wavelengths/we are fuelled by a different kind of engine.

   The trouble is, when we spend too much time with people who set us off kilter like this, it can drain us of our energy and focus.

   Of course, there are also some people who do find boundaries difficult on a more serious level; people for whom it seems all take and not much give. Be wary of these people and these relationships and be sure to enforce boundaries to protect your time and energy. Try saying things like 'I only have a few minutes before I have to … (insert excuse)'. Resist offering too many solutions; rather, say something like, 'I'm sure you'll come to a solution on your own'.

2. **Notice if you feel resentful or genuinely enthusiastic about the things you agree to do.**

   Very often this is a matter of listening to our gut. You know that nervy, fluttery feeling you get after agreeing to something?

Or the awful 'clenched stomach'? Chances are this is because you agreed out of obligation rather than because you genuinely wanted to. Equally, you'll know when you genuinely want to do something because all you'll feel is gladness and excitement. Learn to tune into these feelings more and understand the difference between them – even keep a diary if it helps. Your instinct is a very powerful thing – learn to trust it more.

3. **Take responsibility for enforcing healthy boundaries.**

   Remember: if what you're doing makes you feel resentful, it's ultimately not the person's fault, it's yours for not enforcing healthy boundaries.

   Many people don't like to ask for favours or even help, but there are some people who will always see what they can get away with! Their attitude is very much: 'She can always say no …' So it's really up to you to protect your time and do just that if you feel uncomfortable doing whatever it is they're asking of you. If you don't, you can't moan afterwards!

Compassionate ways to say 'no' …

How many times have you said 'yes' when inside you're thinking 'no'? Say, for example, if someone invites you to give a talk or presentation on a certain topic – because you're so good at it! (often these requests are wrapped up in a compliment) – or to look after their children, when you have some of your own, or if you'd just take a look at the blog they're writing/put a good word in for them to your boss/coach the under 11s cricket this season …

It's completely counter-intuitive, but so many of us say yes when we mean no. It seems to be human nature and there are myriad reasons we do this: we don't want to be impolite, we don't want to sound unkind, we don't want to never be asked again. And then there is simply because we don't know how to say 'no' without risking all the above happening …

The problem is that saying 'yes' when we mean 'no' can quickly become a bad habit leading to resentment and spreading ourselves too thinly. Most of all, it can be a drastic drain on our time and our resources – and, crucially, our focus.

The good news is there are several ways to say 'no' well and with compassion. So next time you feel 'yes' on the tip of your tongue, when really you want to say 'no', try one of the following:

- I'm really sorry I can't help, but I know who can.
- Not for me this time, but thanks for asking.
- I'd like to but I'm snowed under at the moment. I'd love to help another time though; can you come back to me in a month?
- I can't help with this, I'm afraid. But let me tell you what I CAN do.
- I'd love to see you, but for this month I'm prioritizing my health/work/kids … can we do next month?
- (And sometimes it's perfectly ok to say…) I'd love to but I can't.

> **66 Every time we say yes to something we aren't really engaged with, that we don't really want to do, we are taking time away from saying yes to the things and the people we love. 99**
>
> Brigid Schulte, author of *Overwhelmed*

When to say 'no'

If knowing 'how' to say no is a skill, then so is knowing *when* to say no – in fact, arguably, more so. Of course, ultimately only you can make the 'yes' or 'no' decision but, ironically, it's usually when we're pressed for time or harassed that we say 'yes' when we mean 'no': we're so caught up in the moment we don't stop to think which is the right answer.

The truth is that saying 'no' does not only have to be when we're overloaded with stuff to do, and already feeling overcommitted, it can also be because what we're being asked to do is not actually worth our time and energy in terms of what we get out of it. Time management gurus and coaches call this your 'return value', and learning to weigh it up is a key component to Real Focus. Ask yourself, how much energy and time is this going to take? What will you get in return? (This doesn't necessarily have to mean financial gain either, it can mean in terms of fulfillment/career progression/a stepping stone towards a bigger goal or even how it benefits others. Not all favours carry equal value, even to the beneficiary, after all.) All in all, using 'no' and 'yes' well means getting into the habit of asking yourself: is this a good use of my time? Before you say either!

REAL PEOPLE

"I realized I had to make the most of now" *– Kate*

'It was last year that things reached a head. I'd been at home with my twins for a few years (they're now 6) and I felt like I should really do something – but everything came at once.

I got a job working for the council doing adult learning courses and then felt obliged to take on the PTA since nobody else wanted to do it. This also led me to becoming chair, but again, I felt obligated take on this role because nobody else wanted to do it. I felt sorry for them and took on the role out of guilt, really.

By Christmas I was working and doing the PTA, spending my weekends and evenings on the computer and rushing around trying to get everything done. I felt I was doing nothing well.

My family life was suffering as a result. I had arranged for us to go to Lapland and planned all sorts of family stuff. Amidst this I continued doing work prep for the courses I was taking. I bought the twins some books for Christmas, but by the time it got to January I hadn't managed to read them anything. I simply hadn't had time to do any family stuff and also fell ill with a bad cold that I couldn't seem to shake off.

By the time we went to Lapland, I couldn't enjoy it properly because I felt so run down. It was a case of thinking and feeling like I had time to fill and then it going from zero to a hundred miles an hour within a few months.

I began to realize that I was putting this stress on myself. I wanted to be able to just watch a film with the kids in the evenings, but felt like I just didn't have the time. I felt terrible saying no to them. Then I realized that, actually, I didn't have to work in the evenings and the weekends.

I felt guilty at the thought of leaving the PTA, but then I thought why do I feel guilty? There are plenty of people at the school who could be doing this stuff.

I then started to resent it and thought this is illogical and madness – why do it if I'm going to feel so bitter about it?

So I decided to step down from being the chair of the PTA, offering to help only with the things that I wanted to help with and in my time. Willingly.

As soon as I did this, it was like a weight off my shoulders. I feel so much better about it all. I am a nicer person, the kids see me more, I have a better relationship with my husband.

It's about being realistic and putting my family first. I feel like my kids are getting older and there will be a time when they don't want to do things with me, so I have to make the most of it now.'

INVEST IN YOUR TIME

Time is our most valuable commodity, but we so often waste it or don't use it efficiently. If our time management is wrong then everything else tends to feel wrong too. For example, if we're constantly late for things, misjudge how long it will take to do things or just plain old lazy, leaving deadlines to the very last minute, it makes us stressy and panicked – two great enemies of Real Focus.

CHUNK IT DOWN!

Chunking is setting aside a chunk of time for a specific task and doing ONLY that for the time allotted – no emails, no phone calls, just the one task. If it helps, set a timer.

Sometimes, all you need to set you on the right track are good ideas. So, be inspired to take control of your time:

SHÁÁ WASMUND ON HOW TO INVEST IN YOUR TIME

Ask yourself regularly how you want to spend your time – what is most valuable to you.

'If we think of our lives like a rose garden, we can see that in order to get the maximum nutrients in – i.e. to make our lives work as well as possible for ourselves – we need to prune back. Cutting back what we're never going to do (you know, those things on your to-do list that are never going to get done!). But it can also mean cutting back junk and clutter, paperwork, clothes, anything that is making your life more complicated.'

Schedule, schedule, schedule!

'What gets scheduled gets done. What is the one thing you really want to do? Schedule it for a month away – a month is plenty of time to plan and make time for it.'

Break down big projects into smaller tasks to be done with closer deadlines.

'So, rather than "I have to write this 10,000 word report by the end of the month", make a deadline for 3,000 of it to be done in a week's time and so on.'

Sometimes, do nothing.

'Good ideas need time to percolate, and it is in the spaces of sitting quietly that often the best ones come.'

Eat that frog!

'Coined by the Canadian entrepreneur Brian Tracy – "eat that frog" basically means identifying the one thing you're dreading doing or have been putting off forever and getting it out of the way at the beginning of the day. It's hard to focus on anything when we have something tricky hanging over us, so "eat that frog!" and do it, so you can get on with the rest of your day.'

'Batch tasks.'

'Batching tasks just means grouping similar tasks into batches – it avoids that constant "moving from one type of task to another", which can be mentally draining and lead to a lack of focus.'

As we said in Chapter 1, unfortunately it doesn't matter how good your focus is (before or after reading this book!). We can't stretch actual time for you; we can't create extra hours in the day. However, just as there are clever ways to invest your time (some of which are outlined above), there are also clever ways to make your time go further. Mark Forster's 'End Effect' is one such way ...

MARK FORSTER ON THE END EFFECT

'Good teachers know to go through the most important things at the beginning and the end of a lesson, when concentration is at its highest.

Lessons at school are split up into 50-minute chunks for a good reason. If we do work for a set amount of *time – meaning we're working towards that goal – we can see the end: we get the "End Effect". The End Effect is simply how our work becomes much more focused and concentrated at the end.*

We can improve our productivity and lessen our sense of overwhelm if we work in short bursts, creating the End Effect more often throughout the day, making the very most of concentrated and focused work.

If we make those periods short – say 20 minutes – we get the End Effect for those whole 20 minutes. (Also, break for lunch and dinner, and have a mid morning break and an afternoon break.) You'll find that all the time you're working is concentrated time. Actually set an alarm and when the "ping" goes off literally stop, even if you're mid-sentence.'

We hope that having read this chapter you feel more in control of your time and therefore more focused. We hope you can see that 'reclaiming your time' does not mean having more of it, but using what you do have, better. Hopefully you have taken specific time-management tips from this chapter that you can start trying out right away: good boundaries, time-chunking, creating the End Effect and so on. However, the most crucial thing we'd like you to take away – the 'big picture' thing if you like – is that in order to truly manage our time well and become more focused, we need to firstly find out what we value most, then do more of it. We at *Psychologies* believe that this really is the key to a happier life – and who doesn't want that? The cherry on the top then, is being 'present' in that life and savouring every second. Something that we're about to explore in Chapter 9.

ASK YOURSELF

 How do I see my time? In terms of a 24-hour space? A 9–5 then an evening? Or a whole week?

 Have I ever sat down and logged where my time goes? Could I try this?

 What would I like to see more/less of in my day which would enhance my life?

 How can I get more 'End Effect' into my day?

CHAPTER 9

BE PRESENT

B y now, we hope you have a much clearer idea about what Real Focus is and how to start cultivating it. The hard part now is going to be staying focused when it matters. This is where being present is really important – besides anything else, how can you enjoy your life if you're not 'present' in it?

WHAT DOES BEING 'PRESENT' REALLY MEAN?

It's a good question. 'Be present' after all could sound like one of those airy-fairy concepts like 'be authentic'. You may be thinking, 'but I *am* "present" – I am here, reading this book! What's the difference between that and being truly "present" anyway?'

Just like 'Real Focus', being present/living in the moment/ being 'there' – whatever you want to call it – is a feeling and experience that is individual to us all. However, as a guide, it means watching your life as it unfolds rather than projecting into the future or harking back to the past. It means noticing and appreciating what's there rather than what's not. See, when you're trying to complete a task but half your mind's on that awkward conversation you're going to have to have with your Mum at the end of the day? That's not 'being present' (and yet, we spend an alarming amount of time worrying about things exactly like this). Focusing 100 per cent on what is right there in front of you IS.

If we think about it, this moment, right now, is all we can count on, it is all we have. We can't do anything about the past and we can't predict the future, so it makes sense to invest all we have in the here and now rather than pour energy into thinking about situations we have no control over. When we start to do that, we will find our lives feel richer and more vivid; we will feel calmer, more grateful for what we've got and, you guessed it, more focused.

WHY IS BEING PRESENT SO IMPORTANT?

We have outlined some of the benefits above, but consider also the fact that just as being overwhelmed causes our brain to shrink (as we covered in Part One), learning how to focus on the current moment, actually causes it to grow.

In *Overwhelmed*, Brigid Schulte interviewed Harvard neuroscientist Britta Holzel. Holzel is leading one of the many studies of the effects of being present on the brain, and she and her team found that after eight weeks of meditating and practising yoga, the grey matter of her study participants actually grew. This doesn't mean all the stresses of life went away – they were just counteracted by the effects of the meditation and yoga, both of which are practices in being present. Holzel says in Schulte's book:

> 'The point is, the overwhelm never goes away. But you can change how you think about it: pausing and noticing it without passing judgment or reacting to it … Changing your thinking makes your brain grow. And a bigger brain, more sizzling neurons means more grey matter to think and make decisions more clearly …'

It may have already occurred to you that another word for the practice being described here is 'Mindfulness'. There can't be many people who haven't come across this term yet, but what does it actually mean? How do you do it and why is it so good?

66**With mindfulness you realize there's no need to rush to the next moment, it will come automatically. And you will probably get more done by concentrating on what's happening right now anyway.** 99

Britta Holzel, quoted in *Overwhelmed* by Brigid Schulte

153

WHAT IS MINDFULNESS ANYWAY?

When you hear the word 'mindfulness', what comes ... well ... to mind? Breathing deeply? Sitting in the lotus position? Being in 'the here and now'? Whilst all these things can and do play a part, there is actually a lot more to the practice of mindfulness. When mastered, it can be a hugely important tool for Real Focus and productivity; so much so that all over the country, everyone from CEOs, to sportspeople and entire corporations, are signing up to classes in mindfulness to improve everything from revenue to customer relations to the general dynamism of their staff.

In order to understand what mindfulness really is and how to practise it, we need to understand that as human beings we have basically two mental states:

1. **Default Mode Network**: We spend a lot of time in this state! This is the 'mind wandering' state; where we are 'elsewhere'. It's when we're ruminating about the past (I really wish I hadn't said that) and worrying about the future (what if I get made redundant/what will become of me?). We are no longer present or concentrating on the stuff that's right in front of us in the here and now.

   The exciting thing is that there is another side to the Default Mode Network that, if tapped into, could reap huge rewards in terms of focus. When our mind wanders, after all, it can sometimes be for the good. We can be disappearing into our imagination, dreams and memories – the DMN is therefore also the place where amazing creativity COULD happen if it wasn't clogged up with the rumination and self-criticism – what psychologists call 'Generating Scenarios'. When we're doing this, we cannot access the amazing capacity of the Default Mode Network.

2. **The Attentional Network:** This is recruited when we decide to pay attention moment by moment – when we focus just on what we're doing. When we are truly 'there'.

NB: When we're practising mindfulness, we're switching between these two networks.

TAMARA RUSSELL'S SIX STEP GUIDE TO PRACTISING MINDFULNESS

1. *'FOCUS: We start to focus on something; we try to concentrate on what we're doing. This needs to be a deliberate choice.*

2. *MONITORING: We notice when our mind starts to wander – which it will! By practising mindfulness we start to become more sensitive to the switch between "I'm paying attention, I'm not paying attention". We deliberately cultivate our ability to notice when we've left one mode and gone to another.*

3. *CHOICE: We then realize we have a choice: to remain in the so-called Default Mode Network (activated during mind-wandering) or to move back to the Attentional Network (engaged when we choose to focus). As we get better at this, we spend less time in the mind-wandering loop, OR we manage to harness the capacity of the Default Mode Network to dream, imagine and be creative (so it depends on the sort of task we're doing). Remember it's not about having NO mind-wandering, but rather using the resource of our brain most efficiently.*

4. *SHIFTING: You gently and without judgement bring the attention back. This promotes "self-mastery" – in*

that we begin to notice and be aware of our emotions, thoughts and how the mind is behaving and we "master" the art of bringing the focus back in whatever we're doing. There are ways we can help ourselves to do this: by concentrating on our breath or bringing the attention back to the body: how does our body feel? What sensations are right here right now? The body will always bring you home. The body and the breath are sure-fire tickets to the present moment and are always with you. Shifting your attention to these as often as you can during the day is one type of 'informal' mindfulness training.

5. **INTENTION:** In order to engage the Attentional Network and shift back your attention to the object you have chosen, effort is required. Because it is effortful, it helps if there is some understanding of the "why" behind the activity. Why is this meaningful for you? Ask yourself, what's more important to me right now? Thinking about the email I need to send, or listening to my daughter tell me about her school play? For example. When we find meaning and have a strong intention, it's much easier to focus.

6. **MOTIVATION:** We realize that we didn't get where we are in this new "focused" Attentional Network state through screwing our face up and going "I will focus, I will focus!" We got there through a disciplined attempt to focus and a gentle but firm management of the inevitable lack of focus – mind-wandering. When we start to have some success with this, we are encouraged and this can help motivate us to keep going or try to use these shifts of attention under more extreme circumstances. We understand, I can choose; we've asked ourselves, is it

useful to ruminate? Is it useful to do this thing or more useful to do the other? We have reduced the activity in the mind of the "should monkey" ("future thinking" based on the idea that I "should" or "shouldn't" do something) and the mental monkey that likes to analyze "Why did I? Why didn't I?" – harking back to the past and going over and over previous decisions. When we can start to tame these mental monkeys, only engaging them when it is helpful to us, we start to get results, notice more ease and spaciousness in the mind and are motivated to keep on practising.'

> 66 **Getting out of the overwhelm, is waking up to the fact that time is fleeting … life is going to be over so quickly and the only thing we really can do is recognize that today is an amazingly beautiful day.** 99

Brigid Schulte, author of *Overwhelmed*

WHAT TO DO WHEN WE'RE OVERWHELMED 'IN THE MOMENT'

It's all very well us knowing how to practise mindfulness, but what about in that moment when we're overwhelmed and stressed? How can we bring the focus back when we're in a head-spin?

Know your triggers

Your triggers are the things that set you off into the mind-spin. The things that always set you off course. You will know what yours are, but classic triggers are things like:

- being late;
- being on a deadline;
- your system breaking down (more of this in Chapter 10).

This could mean something that disturbs the usual order of things – you've left your car lights on all night and now the battery is flat, for example. These little things are sent to test us and can very easily set all our best intentions to be mindful totally off course. They are times when the flow is disturbed and we're launched into an unpredictable state of affairs. The main thing is recognizing that this has happened (monitoring – see step 2 in Tamara Russell's six-step guide above), but also asking yourself what the 'pay off' is of going down that unfocused road and whether regaining your focus could have a bigger pay off? For example, why are you always 10 minutes late? Could it be that you hate being bored and turning up somewhere having time to spare? This is all very understandable, but what are the consequences of your lateness? Irritating other people/being stressed because you arrive in a flap/not enjoying the moment because you're too busy stressing about being late? Weigh it up. Is it worth it?

> 66 **When I feel overwhelmed and have lost my focus, I take myself outside; I change my environment. Then I write**

everything down that I have to do and I decide, right: I'm going to focus on this one thing. One thing at a time. "

Sháá Wasmund, MBE, speaker, entrepreneur and author

Tamara Russell suggests that bringing your focus back when you've lost it in the moment can also be about creating new habits. It's very easy to create a bad habit – we get in a bad 'loop' and can't seem to get out of it – so very often simple, practical amendments to our situation can really help.

1. Check how many windows you have open.
2. Pick a designated amount of time to do a task.
3. Switch off audio and visual signifiers if you have 'beeps' when you've got a new email or pop-ups on your screen, otherwise the brain has to adjust to take it into consideration and then it takes time for you to get back your concentration.

In general, remember that creating good habits and breaking bad ones comes down to awareness – to *noticing* things more. It is only when we notice how certain things or people or situations make us feel, after all, that we can make choices (to form a new good habit or stop a bad one). How do you feel when you drink alcohol on two consecutive nights, for example? Equally, if you make a commitment to getting some exercise every day, what are the benefits? How does it make you feel? Keep a diary if it helps to get you into the *habit* of noticing!

In fact, awareness really is the first step to creating habits. It gives us power and autonomy and this is never truer than when we find ourselves at the centre of an overwhelming moment – you know the sort, when your head is spinning? The ability to say 'what's going on here? How is it making me feel?' Then being able to adjust our behaviour accordingly (deciding to do less or more of it) is what makes us more sophisticated than animals. Don't waste this amazing skill we have for adapting and changing our lives for the better. The power really is in your hands, it's just knowing how to use it.

> **66 Being mindful of family time, making a commitment to be there physically and mentally and enjoy life while doing so makes memories possible. 99**
>
> Laura Vanderkam, author and speaker

KNOW WHEN THE GOOD MOMENTS ARE HAPPENING

Very often we are so whipped into a frenzy and obsessed with what we have to do that we don't even recognize the lovely things that are happening right in front of us. Equally, making meaningful moments in our lives does not have to be a big deal, and with a bit of focus we can make them even when we are tight for time and stressed. Feel guilty you don't spend enough 'quality time' with your children? But you don't need to be planning elaborate outings for it to be 'quality time'. A chat whilst you walk to school, or in bed at night for five minutes, can be just as meaningful.

Also, consider that guilt is generally a pretty useless emotion and an enemy of Real Focus.

LAURA VANDERKAM ON THE GUILT TRAP (AND HOW TO GET OUT OF IT)

'We think about "me" time as silly or indulgent but it's really important to take time to ask yourself: is this what I want to be doing in my life? Is this how I want to be living? Try and rid yourself of guilt. Don't assume you have to spend all your time with your children, for example. Kids need to be away from us, they need to fail and get back up, they need independence and to figure out how to use this independence wisely. They don't need to be entertained by us all the time, so that when you do spend time together it's not fuelled by guilt and stress.

Don't think either that everything has to be big and wonderful and grand – you don't need to do something like a trip to the park even to spend "quality" time with the children; just sitting down and having a chat is good, finding the extraordinary in the ordinary. Recognize that you are "present" and don't beat yourself up all the time. How can we enjoy and have proper joyful moments if we're too beaten up with guilt?'

66 What spins us out of control is a lot of fear – about things which probably won't actually come to pass. 99

Brigid Schulte, author of *Overwhelmed*

In summary then, if Real Focus is really about Doing What Matters then mindfulness is the art of being aware that we're doing it. How can we improve upon or, more importantly, enjoy the lives we have if we're not present in them? We hope you can see that this doesn't have to mean going on a mindfulness course, learning meditation or deep breathing, it simply means opening your eyes, ears and heart and noticing. This is practising Real Focus at its simplest level – but as we know, the simple things in life are often the most effective.

REAL PEOPLE
"Yoga helps to give me perspective" – *Marianne*

'A year ago I unexpectedly became a single mum to twin girls and, even though it was wonderful, my life as I knew it was turned upside down. Before it had been all about me – I was able to potter and plan, I was able to relax and things were calm. Now, suddenly working full time and coming home to look after two babies, I had very little mental space or time to myself.

I had practised yoga before and loved it, but now it became my saviour. Yoga is all about me. It's a time when I don't think about anything else and so it's a rest for my brain. Physically it makes me feel strong and it also makes me feel connected to my body. This is because, in order to do the poses, you have to think about your body and what it's doing; you have to think about your breathing – you cannot think of anything else, otherwise you wouldn't be able to do the poses.

Sometimes I am so overwhelmed that I will look at the pile of washing up and panic! Or walk from room to messy room not knowing where to start. It's then that I know I need to do yoga. It gets me out of my head and into my body. It makes me feel stronger internally and more resilient, able to get on with what I need to do. Often, my to-do list is swimming around in my head in a jumble, but after doing yoga, the list becomes a proper organized list and I am able to prioritize. I do it for about 45 minutes to an hour when the girls are in bed or when stress is beginning to manifest itself physically. It gives me perspective – suddenly the "big" problems don't feel so big anymore. Yoga keeps me sane!'

ASK YOURSELF

 How present do you feel in your life? How could you cultivate more 'meaningful moments' or notice when they're there?

 Do you find yourself ruminating about the past or worrying more about the future? How useful do you feel this is? Does it make you feel calmer?

 Are you aware when your mind wanders? Could you make a pact to notice more?

 What are your triggers to slipping into Default Network Mode? Boredom? Feeling that your skills don't meet the task?

CHAPTER 10

EMBRACE SYSTEMS

e hope by this point in the book that you feel better about your focus. We hope that at least we have given you more confidence in your ability to improve it – perhaps you've already started and are already seeing results.

We hope, if nothing else, that we've conveyed to you our core message that, actually, Real Focus is about doing what really matters to YOU most, and that this isn't so hard when you really put your mind to it.

Of course, having goals is a big part of achieving Real Focus. Goals give us a reason for travelling in a certain direction in our lives and spur us on to keep chipping away. However, in this last chapter, we want to explain how even goals aren't that useful if you don't have systems to get you there. Think of goals as the destination, if you like, and systems the mode of transport: it's all very well having your heart set on going to Cornwall, but if the train breaks down, you're screwed!

Writing in *The Guardian* the *Psychologies* columnist Oliver Burkeman said that if you want to succeed, you need systems not goals. Constantly going after goals, he writes, means you exist 'in a state of near-continuous failure' because you are perpetually 'NOT in a state that you've defined as embodying accomplishment or success'.

'A system by contrast,' he says 'is something you do on a regular basis that increases your odds of happiness in the long run.' You may not have the big guns blazing, fist pumping moments so much, but you do have 'a little triumph every day' – which we think sounds a whole lot better.

> # FOCUS ON A 'SYSTEM' RATHER THAN THE GOAL
>
> **By doing this we allow ourselves to concentrate on the things we CAN control (our actions and our efforts) rather than on what we can't – i.e. the outcome. You'll usually find you get to the goal in the end anyway, and you'll have enjoyed the journey too!**

IN PRAISE OF SYSTEMS

Many of us might like to think that being creative types, systems aren't for us. We're far more comfortable flying by the seat of our pants and using our instincts. There is certainly a place for this; as Sháá Wasmund writes in her book *Do Less, Get More*: 'Confidence is the ability to filter out the interference and know what feels right in your heart. And not only know it, but follow it.'

For certain people, gut instinct can be a very good guide. However, not everybody does have the confidence to follow or even recognize their gut instinct and this is why systems can be a safer and more reliable option. Think of systems as the foundations of what you do – freeing up more space in your head for wonderful creativity. Systems give you the freedom to do your best work and also to not continue to make the same mistakes again and again. When you devise a great system, you don't have to think about it again. Also, consider this: gut instinct and systems don't have to be mutually exclusive – you can always use them in tandem.

Systems as habits

If we think of systems as habits it can help to make them sound less scary for one thing! Habits are things that we do often and regularly – but cultivating good ones can make a huge difference to our lives. The psychologist Gretchen Rubin wrote how habits – and how having a sound, solid 'architecture of habits' to support our lives – are crucial to our happiness. It makes sense that if we have habits (or systems to use that other word) that work for us, life is going to feel much easier; think of our systems like the oil that keep the wheels of our life turning. If it's a good quality oil, everything is going to feel much smoother.

Creating your own systems

You can create a system – it's not difficult – the difficult bit is creating a good one! One that works for you. Very often what happens is that we create a system (or fail even to do that) that doesn't work for us but that we keep repeating. For example, never having a space to put our car keys so that we are stressed out looking for them every single morning; or never filing away bank statements so that we have to pay to re-order them when we need them. Why do we do this?! And carry on doing it? It's counter-intuitive. However, understanding why – and (as we touched on in Chapter 9) knowing our triggers – is precisely how we can learn to stop and start creating and using systems that actually make our lives easier.

> ## Q&A WITH MARK FORSTER ON THE PSYCHOLOGY OF SYSTEMS
>
> **'Psychologies:** Human beings can sometimes be slow learners when it comes to creating and keeping systems. It's that thing of never putting our car keys in a safe place so that we're always stressed, trying to find them, or never completing our tax return on time so that we then incur charges. Why do we continue to do this? How can we stop in order to make our lives calmer?

Mark: *These are all examples of poor systems. One of my favourite bits of advice is "Think systems!" That's because we are never going to be really focused until we've sorted out the basic systems by which we run our lives. The clues to watch out for are the words "always" and "never". Never putting our car keys in a safe place. Always being stressed. Never completing our tax returns on time. Whenever you find yourself complaining with either of these words, you can be pretty sure that you have a faulty system.*

Psychologies: But why do we continue to use systems which don't work – what's the pay off for us? Why do we do it? And how can we shift our focus to coming up with systems that DO work.

Mark: *I could produce all sorts of psychological jargon to explain why, but I think the simple answer is that when something goes wrong it takes less time to do a work-around than to sit down and work out why it went wrong. If it's a question of taking 5 minutes to do a work-around versus taking 15 minutes to design a new system, the work-around is going to win every time. Never mind that we'll being doing the work-around several times a day for the rest of our working life, while designing a new system is a one-off job.*

The remedy is that whenever you catch yourself saying "always" or "never" you should make a note to sit down at the earliest possible opportunity to design a better system. Sometimes systems are easy to design and sometimes they are harder, but the time spent on them is never wasted.

Psychologies: Can you give us a baby-step guide to how to create a good system?

Mark: The first step is always to work out what your existing system is. For instance, many people use something like the following system to handle email:

1. *Download ten emails.*
2. *Take action on five.*
3. *Leave the remaining five for later.*
4. *Repeat many times throughout the day.*

Can you see that this system is inevitably going to produce a backlog of email? What would be a better system? Well, almost anything really! (See Mark's "Inbox Zero" approach in Chapter 4.)'

TRY 'NO ZERO' DAYS

A 'No Zero Day' is basically the policy of not letting a day go past without doing something towards whatever project you have on the go. Real Focus is often about taking small, regular baby steps towards your big goal, so even if it's 'make a call' or 'spend 20 minutes on it' as long as it is moving you towards your goal, then that counts as a 'No Zero Day'.

We hope, after reading this chapter, that you can see how systems act as the framework or architectural structure holding up not just your ability to focus, but your whole life. Spend time on creating sound systems in your working and your home life, and you will reap huge rewards (there's that 'reward value' thing again): things will go more smoothly, you'll save more time, be more efficient and, ultimately, just enjoy things more. It's really when we feel in harmony like this that we are able to focus to the best of our ability. That's it in a nutshell, really: great systems = better focus = happier us.

"A simple change to my system changed everything"

– Stephanie

'I was in the middle of a meeting when the taxman called. 'If you don't pay, we're coming round to take your furniture' – it was *that* bad. The thing was, I knew I didn't owe the taxman much, it was merely a case of getting my receipts in on time – why had I not done it?

I rang up my friend in tears, she said "you do this every year, Stephanie". I felt so ashamed, like a total idiot. The stress it created was so unnecessary. I rang up my accountant, he said 'well I can't do anything until you've sent me your receipts'.

When I got home that night, I did them and of course realized it wasn't that hard! Why did I never do it? I decided I'd never do this again. I thought about the pay off for not doing it: it was that it was boring, I didn't want to do it and also there was the fear that the taxman might say I owed lots of money which I didn't have, even though deep down I knew if I'd just organized myself, I didn't owe that much.

My so-called system was to throw all my receipts into an envelope – so that I had a year's worth of receipts – it was so overwhelming when it came to doing my annual tax return. I realized that this system – the non-system – was causing me so much stress that I couldn't carry on like this. I called a friend of mine who is an accounts clerk and we came up with an arrangement: once a month I'd put all my receipts in an envelope and send them to her and she'd do the book-keeping for £100 a year. It was so simple yet so effective. Once I'd arranged this, I felt the stress lift like a weight off my shoulders – why had I not organized this before?!

It's a small thing but now I feel like a proper grown up and in control. Asking myself why I continued to use a system that didn't work for me and resolving to do something about it changed everything!'

ASK YOURSELF

 Do you have systems for things to make your life easier?

 Do the ones that exist actually serve you well? Or do you continue to use a system that doesn't work/ continue to be stuck in bad habits?

 Could you put aside a bit of time to note down which systems in your life work for you and which don't? You could split them up into areas of your life: financial/ personal/the children/fitness and literally make a list.

 How could you build a new architecture of habits that will build useful/successful systems?

WHAT NEXT?

Congratulations on getting to the end of *Real Focus* – so, how do you feel? Inspired? Surprised by what you've learned about yourself and Real Focus? Chances are, you'll now want to close this book, let it all percolate, and come back to the bits you enjoyed the most or that you felt were the most relevant or helpful. Perhaps you've been making notes as you've read, and now want to go over them; perhaps you want to give this book to a friend.

However you've used or read this book, we just hope that you've got something from it. Also, of course, your journey towards Real Focus does not end here – in fact, we hope this marks your beginning.

Let's face it, anybody can read a book like this, find it interesting but then never think about their focus again. We don't want that to happen! We want this to be a 'way in'/the catalyst for your talking about better focus, how you might achieve it, and how it could enhance your life.

We'd love this book to be your 'Focus Bible' from now on – a place to go back to again and again if in need of motivation, ideas, strategies, or just a little bit of inspiration on those days when you feel your focus is flagging (because every single one of us has them).

Each one of you will have your own reasons for picking up this book and we really hope you've enjoyed reading it as much as we have putting it together. We hope you can see that Real Focus is not about fancy time-management skills, learning to concentrate for hours on end or even getting more done. Real Focus is simply about living a life you want, having more time to do the sorts of things that bring you joy and fulfillment. All it boils down to, really, is that cultivating more focus in your life naturally leads to cultivating more happiness, and who doesn't want that? Here's to better, greater Real Focus today and in the future!

ABOUT PSYCHOLOGIES

Psychologies is a magazine read by those who want to lead a fulfilling life, who want to live a life on their own terms, however you choose to define it. *Psychologies* helps you discover what 'life success' looks like for you – from the inside out.

We're on a mission to find out from the best experts and latest research in psychology how we can all lead happier and more fulfilling lives. *Psychologies* is not about striving to do more but rather finding ways to BE more. Who are you? And what do you really want? These are questions we're always asking ourselves. *Psychologies* magazine is about being the best you; and we mean being in an active way: becoming the best you can be, the happiest and the most fulfilled you.

We focus on helping you understand yourself and the world around you, by gathering the latest, most compelling thinking and translating it into practical wisdom that can support you as you create the life that works for you.

Real Focus is written by journalist and novelist, Katy Regan. After 10 years as staff writer and columnist on various women's magazines, Katy became Commissioning Editor of *Marie-Claire* magazine. In 2008, she left the world of magazines to write novels. She has to date published four novels with Harper Collins, the latest being *The Story of You*. She also writes journalism regularly for *Psychologies* and most other national magazines and newspapers including *Stella magazine*, *Good Housekeeping* and *Marie-Claire*. Visit her author website at www.katyregan.com and follow her on Twitter @katyreganwrites. Katy lives in Hertfordshire with her son.

REFERENCES

CHAPTER 1

1. *Forbes* magazine, October 2014. http://www.forbes.com/sites/
travisbradberry/2014/10/08/multitasking-damages-your-brain-
and-career-new-studies-suggest/.

CHAPTER 2

1. 'The Busy Trap', Tom Krieder, 30 June 2012, *New York Times*,
http://opinionator.blogs.nytimes.com/2012/06/30/the-busy-
trap/?_r=0.
2. Ibid.

CHAPTER 3

1. 'How the internet is making us stupid', Nicholas Carr, *The
Telegraph*, 27 August 2010, http://www.telegraph.co.uk/
technology/internet/7967894/How-the-Internet-is-making-us-
stupid.html.
2. Ibid.

Notes

Notes

Notes